# Ultimate!

# WALL STREET

# TRIVIA

## 1001
### Fun and Fascinating Facts

Scott Paul Frush

Marshall Rand Publishing
P.O. Box 701128
Plymouth, Michigan 48170

Printed in the United States of America

*Although every precaution was made in preparation of this book, the publisher
and author assume no responsibility for omissions or errors biographical or
otherwise.*

Frush, Scott Paul
    Ultimate Wall Street Trivia / Scott Paul Frush

pBook 13-Digit ISBN: 978-0-9888254-7-5

# Contents

# About the Author

Scott Paul Frush, CFA, CFP is founder and managing director of Frush Financial Group (www.Frush.com), a Northville, Michigan registered investment adviser, and a past instructor of finance at the University of Michigan. He is the publisher of the *ETF Market Watch* newsletter and blog as well as the founder and host of ETF Professor TV. He has helped investors protect, grow, and insure their wealth for nearly two decades.

Scott earned the Chartered Financial Analyst (CFA) and Certified Financial Planner (CFP) designations as well as various insurance and securities licenses. Frush holds an MBA from the University of Notre Dame and a bachelors from Eastern Michigan University.

Scott is the author of ten other books—seven on investments and three on trivia. His latest investing book is titled *The Strategic ETF Investor* (shown in the author photo), published by McGraw-Hill.

# CHAPTER 1

# PEOPLE, PLACES, AND THINGS

*Investigating Landmark Leaders and
Landmark Destinations*

*" If past history was all that is needed to play the
game of money, the richest people would be librarians. "*

**- WARREN BUFFETT**

*"To be in the game, you have to endure the pain. "*

**- GEORGE SOROS**

(1)     A sculpture of what animal was originally placed in front of the NYSE and later moved to its current location in Bowling Green?

(2)     Finish the title of the highly popular book by Burton Malkiel; *A* _____ *Walk Down Wall Street.*

(3)     How did John D. Rockefeller make his fortune?

(4)     In what year did construction on the New York World Trade Center begin? (a) 1966, (b) 1969, (c) 1972, (d) 1975, (e) 1977

(5)     Name the highly regarded and influential banking analyst that made the questionable prediction that scores of municipalities will go bankrupt and muni bonds fall into default.

(6)     This financial giant began his career as a Staten Island ferryman. Name him.

(7)     This Wall Street leader is credited with financing the Union during the Civil War by selling U.S. Treasury bonds in Europe. Name this unsung hero.

(8)     What noted Yale economist reassured worried investors in October 1929 that their "money was safe" on Wall Street just before the stock market crash?

(9)     Which family controlled more than 60% of the voting stock of Dow Jones & Company when it agreed to sell the company to News Corp in 2007?

(10)    Who is known as the "Oracle of Omaha"?

(11) Who founded Electronic Data Systems (EDS) in Plano, Texas in 1962?

(12) Who was the very first female member (in 1967) of the New York Stock Exchange?

(13) Alcoa, Comcast, and Toll Brothers are all headquartered in which state?

(14) George Bush, Sr. described the economic policies of what fellow GOP presidential candidate as "voodoo economics"?

(15) How many years in prison did Bernard Madoff get for his Ponzi scheme conviction?

(16) Located in the financial center of London, England, this major "street" was established by Italian bankers from Lombardi. Name this street that is the counterpart to Wall Street.

(17) The past accolades of which person include running the hedge fund Traxis Partners, holding the title of "chief global strategist" for Morgan Stanley, named by *Institutional Investor* magazine to its "All-America Research Team" 10 times, and called "the ultimate big-picture man" at *Smart Money* magazine?

(18) This person is not only the founder and former chairman of The Vanguard Group, but also credited with the creation of the first index fund available to individual investors. Name him.

(19) Who succeeded Bill Gates as CEO of Microsoft?

(20)  What is the name for the building located at 40 Wall Street named for a wealthy American family? (Hint: The Apprentice)

(21)  Which economist is credited with inventing the "curve" that became a cornerstone of Reaganomics?

(22)  Which Wall Street financier was known as "the adviser to presidents"?

(23)  Who preceded Alan Greenspan as Federal Reserve chairman?

(24)  William K. Vanderbilt is recognized for building what iconic "garden" in New York City?

(25)  According to *Forbes*, in 2011 John Hammergren was the highest compensated CEO of a Fortune 500 company having earned over $130 million for the year. Name his employer.

(26)  Fox News Channel is owned by News Corporation of Australia. Who founded News Corporation?

(27)  Henry Varnum Poor and John Moody established the foundation for what type of company during the 19th-century?

(28)  Name the Federal Reserve chairman as of early 2013.

(29)  This CEO is best known for his role in the widely reported corruption scandal that led to the downfall of Enron. Name him.

(30) Name the first African American owned NYSE member firm.

(31) What company did Billy Durant establish in 1911 after he was forced out of General Motors for the first time?

(32) What surprising educational impairment did Cornelius Vanderbilt suffer from?

(33) Which two financial tycoons endowed a now prestigious university in Pittsburgh, Pennsylvania?

(34) Which well-known portfolio manager runs the PIMCO Total Return Fund, the world's largest bond mutual fund?

(35) Who was the first serving U.S. president to visit the floor of the New York Stock Exchange?

(36) Who was the IMF managing director accused of sexual assault in 2011?

(37) Aside from being CEOs of technology companies, what do Mark Zuckerberg, Bill Gates, Michael Dell, and Steve Jobs all have in common?

(38) Hewlett-Packard was founded in 1939 in Palo Alto by Bill Hewlett and Dave Packard. In what specific structure was the company established?

(39) How did Cornelius Vanderbilt make his fortune?

(40) Name the popular research report published by Marc Faber.

(41) Name the German leader who was front and center during the European financial crisis centering on Greece.

(42) Name the Merrill Lynch CEO ousted in part for spending over $1 million to redecorate his office during the financial crisis.

(43) What artist sings the song "Like a Rock" during Chevy commercials?

(44) What did Facebook CEO Mark Zuckerberg do the day after taking his company public and raising his wealth to more than $19 billion?

(45) When this legendary person died, his obituary in the *Wall Street Journal* read "There will be no successor to him." Name this person.

(46) Who are the two founders of Microsoft?

(47) Who hosted *Wall Street Week* for 32 years until a shakeup in 2002?

(48) Who was the very first chairperson of the Securities and Exchange Commission?

(49) Banks KeyCorp, Fifth Third, and Huntington are all headquartered in which state?

(50) How did John Jacob Astor make his fortune?

(51) Richard Branson founded what airline company in 1984?

(52) In 1909, this person offered to sell his company—now considered an icon of American manufacturing—for $8 million to the fledgling General Motors. Name this person.

(53) Name the three states that boast at least 50 headquarters of Fortune 500 companies.

(54) The Du Pont family made its original fortune in what business enterprise?

(55) What distinction does David Clarkson hold?

(56) What investment bank was Michael Bloomberg affiliated with before launching his own firm, Bloomberg Investments?

(57) Which Boston-based private equity firm was founded in 1984 by Mitt Romney, T. Coleman Andrews III, and Eric Kriss?

(58) Who is the founder and CEO of Oracle Corporation and one of the top ten richest persons in the world in 2012 according to *Forbes* magazine?

(59) Who traded a Volkswagen Beetle to his brother in exchange for his brother's half interest in what was once called DomiNick's?

(60) The character Gordon Gekko from the movie *Wall Street* is based at least in part on which Wall Street titan for the famous speech he delivered where he said; "I think greed is healthy. You can be greedy and still feel good about yourself."?

(61) Who was the well-respected Citigroup Salomon Smith Barney telecom analyst that touted—much to his demise—Worldcom stock in the early 2000s?

(62) Biogen, Panera Bread, and Staples are all headquartered in which state?

(63) In addition to the United States Supreme Court building, which other prominent American historical building closely resembles the well-preserved Roman temple of Maison Carree located in Nimes, France?

(64) Jabil Circuit, AutoNation, and Office Depot are all headquartered in which state?

(65) Nicknamed by *TIME* magazine as the "Arabian Warren Buffett," this Saudi investor once held approximately half of his wealth in Citigroup just prior to the 2008 financial crisis. Name him.

(66) The Gap, Williams-Sonoma, and Visa are all headquartered in which U.S. city?

(67) What is the name of the tallest building with a Wall Street address?

(68) Which CEO and his wife founded the largest U.S. foundation as ranked by asset size?

(69) Which company is the largest nuclear power generator in the United States?

(70) Who was known as the "penny stock king" of the 1950s?

(71) Who was the very first African-American member (in 1970) of the New York Stock Exchange?

(72) This person is most remembered for his involvement in "junk bonds" during the 1970s and 1980s and being indicted on 98 counts of racketeering and securities fraud in 1989 as the result of an insider trading investigation. Name him.

(73) Born March 13, 1956, James "Jamie" Dimon is the CEO of which Wall Street company as of 2013?

(74) Lee Iacocca was fired from the presidency of which company?

(75) Men's Wearhouse, Waste Management, and Baker Hughes are all headquartered in which U.S. city?

(76) The actual street called Wall Street runs along the East River. Between what two streets does Wall Street begin and end?

(77) This business magnate and investor owns the NBA's Dallas Mavericks, Landmark Theatres, and Magnolia Pictures. Name him.

(78) This financial giant—typically associated with Pittsburg—was actually born in Scotland. Name him.

(79) What mutual fund did Peter Lynch manage that gained him significant accolades and fame?

(80) Which financial news and services website did Jim Cramer co-found in 1996?

(81) Which former New Jersey governor started and eventually bankrupted investment firm MF Global?

(82) Who were the first three American billionaires of the 20th-century?

(83) Carl Quintanilla is a news anchor for which cable network?

(84) Corrections Corp. of America, Dollar General Corp., and Ruby Tuesday, Inc. are all headquartered in which state?

(85) Dick Bove is an influential analyst that follows which group of companies in the U.S.?

(86) Lifelong friends Ben Cohen and Jerry Greenfield started what company—now a division of the British-Dutch Unilever conglomerate—in 1978 in downtown Burlington, Vermont?

(87) The Du Pont family built its empire predominately in which U.S. state?

(88) This person became the very first female member of an exchange in 1935 when she joined the Commodities Exchange. Name her.

(89) Starting in 1985, this retailer became the richest person in the United States. Name him.

(90) Which Italian American was elected chairman and CEO of the New York Stock Exchange in 1985, but forced out in the mid-2000s?

(91) Which CEO engineered HP's $25 billion takeover of Compaq in 2000?

(92) Which two financial giants died in the same year—that being 1937?

(93) Who wrote the book *Business @ the Speed of Thought: Succeeding in the Digital Economy* released in 2000?

(94) Caterpillar, Walgreen Co., and Sears Holdings are all headquartered in which state?

(95) What is the official street address for the New York Stock Exchange?

(96) Lockheed Martin, Marriott Intl., and Legg Mason are all headquartered in which state?

(97) Stock analyst Roger Babson is remembered as being the sole person to predict what disastrous event?

(98) This American investor and author was the co-founder of the Quantum Fund with George Soros and creator of a prominent international commodities index that bears his name. Name this person typically seen wearing a bowtie.

(99) Duke Energy, Goodrich Corp., and Lowe's Companies are all headquartered in which state?

(100) What do Steve Jobs, Steve Wozniak, and Ronald Wayne have in common?

(101) Who wrote the book titled *The Wealth of Nations*?

(102) Which company is the last remaining major investment bank with a physical location on Wall Street?

(103) Which veteran and much respected co-anchor of CNBC's morning "Squawk on the Street" show died unexpectedly in 2011?

(104) Which well-known anchor with CNBC wrote the 2005 book titled *Tide: Why Tax Cuts Are the Key to Prosperity and Freedom*?

(105) Actor Dennis Haysbert portrayed baseball player Pedro Cerrano in the *Major League* film trilogy. He is also the official spokesperson for which company?

(106) Fisher Scientific Intl. and Timberland Co. are headquartered in which state?

(107) How did Andrew Carnegie make his fortune?

(108) Microsoft founder Bill Gates dropped out of what university in 1975?

(109) Which chairman of General Motors was named "Man of the Year" by *TIME* magazine in 1956?

(110) This leading financial journalist began her career with CNBC in 1995 as the first journalist to report live from the floor of the New York Stock Exchange. Name this NYU educated Italian American.

(111) What mega-mogul CEO managed a baseball team for one day?

(112) What company did Steve Jobs found after losing a power struggle with the board of directors of Apple in 1984?

(113) Which financial tycoon endowed a university in Nashville, Tennessee?

(114) Which Wall Street investment banking firm did Michael Milken make his fame?

(115) Who founded Amazon.com in 1994?

# CHAPTER 2

# EXCHANGES, ECONOMY, AND MARKETS

*Uncovering the Foundations of Wall Street*

*" I believe in efficient markets. "*

- EUGENE F. FAMA

*" The efficient market is a state of nature dreamed up by theoreticians. "*

- PETER L. BERNSTEIN

(116) Fill in the blank: The New York Stock Exchange is often referred to as "the Big _____".

(117) What does S&P stand for?

(118) In what year did the New York Stock Exchange vote to become a for-profit, public company?

(119) The New York Stock Exchange changed its opening bell from 10am to what time in 1985?

(120) The Dow Jones Industrial Average is named for Charles Henry Dow and what business associate of Dow?

(121) What historical innovation was introduced in 1867 with regards to the stock exchange?

(122) What is the largest stock exchange located outside of New York City?

(123) What is traded over-the-counter on the "third market"?

(124) What major commodities exchange closed its doors in 1976?

(125) What time does the closing bell on the New York Stock Exchange ring to end trading?

(126) National oil companies (NOCs), defined as oil companies fully or majority owned by a national government, produce about what percentage of total global oil output? (a) 10%, (b) 22%, (c) 32%, (d) 52%

(127)   In what year did the Dow Jones Industrial Average first close over 100? (a) 1857, (b) 1877, (c) 1896, (d) 1906, (e) 1919

(128)   In what year was the Standard & Poor's 500 Index established?

(129)   On which day of the week is the crude oil inventory report released by the Energy Information Administration?

(130)   The FTSE 100 Index, also called the FTSE 100, is a share index of the 100 most highly capitalized companies in which country?

(131)   What index, formerly known as the Common Stock Index, was created by the New York Stock Exchange in 1966 to track all common stocks listed on the exchange?

(132)   What is the oldest stock exchange in the United States having been established in 1790?

(133)   What market is characterized by large investors trading among themselves?

(134)   What time does the opening bell on the New York Stock Exchange ring to begin trading?

(135)   True/False: The New York Stock Exchange halts all trading at noon for 30 minutes each day for "lunch".

(136)   In what year was the New York Stock Exchange established?

(137)   Name the largest European trading partner with the United States.

(138)   The Dow Jones Industrial Average was increased to 20 stocks in 1916. How many stocks did the index have prior to this expansion?

(139)   Private consumption + gross investment + government spending + (exports − imports) equals what economic measurement?

(140)   This person became the first salaried chairperson of the New York Stock Exchange in 1972. Name him.

(141)   This exchange is the largest stock exchange in Canada, the third largest in North America, and the seventh largest in the world by market capitalization. Name this stock exchange.

(142)   What is the significance of the date March 16, 1830 for the New York Stock Exchange?

(143)   What type of stocks does the Russell 2000 Index track?

(144)   What type of stocks does the S&P 400 Index track?

(145)   When a company's stock is listed on one or more foreign stock exchanges in addition to its domestic exchange, it is said to be what?

(146)   Prompted by the stock market crash, officials at the NYSE invoked for the first time what rule to halt all trading on October 19, 1987?

(147) Name the only state to have two Federal Reserve Districts within its state border.

(148) Prior to this year, the New York Stock Exchange was closed on Presidential Election Day. In what year did this practice end and the exchange open for the first time on this day?

(149) The Dow Jones Industrial Average hit a high of 381.77 before the crash of 1929. In what year did the Dow finally eclipse the 1929 high?

(150) True/False: The S&P 500 Index includes a financial services company headquartered in Ireland with executive offices in Bermuda.

(151) What was the original name for the American Stock Exchange?

(152) When was the Chicago Board of Trade established? (a) 1799, (b) 1848, (c) 1879, (d) 1899, (e) 1909

(153) Which index is considered the broadest of all indexes for the U.S. equity market, measuring the performance of all U.S. equity securities with readily available price data?

(154) What is the oldest commodities exchange in the United States, having been established in 1848? (a) Chicago Board of Trade, (b) Kansas City Board of Trade, (c) New York Cotton Exchange, (d) Detroit Metal Exchange

(155) What does NASDAQ stand for?

(156)   The Krugerrand is the gold coin issued by what country?

(157)   Which stock exchange changed its name back to the Chicago Stock Exchange in 1993?

(158)   Selling a security you do not own and only borrowed with the objective of buying the same security back at a lower price is referred to as what?

(159)   The Federal Reserve Bank of New York is by far the largest reserve bank. Name the next two largest banks in the Federal Reserve System.

(160)   This economic indicator, released around the first few business days of the month for two months prior, is essentially a compendium of previously announced economic indicators: new orders, jobless claims, money supply, average workweek, building permits, and stock prices. Name this economic indicator.

(161)   Which country is the largest export market for United States goods?

(162)   Which obscure exchange was referred to as the "little board" in the early 1900s?

(163)   Which stock exchange was the first to abolish half-day trading on Saturdays?

(164)   Which U.S. department releases the Housing Starts and Building Permits data?

(165)   About how large was U.S. GDP in trillions for 2012?

(166) Who releases the Initial (jobless) Claims economic indicator each Thursday morning?

(167) How many listings are on the New York Stock Exchange rounded to the nearest hundred?

(168) According to NYSE rules, what percentage fall in one day will close the exchange for the rest of the day?

(169) Approximately when did the New York Stock Exchange surpass the London Stock Exchange as the world's largest exchange?

(170) Started during World War I, what did brokers do to ensure their clerks could easily identify them in a crowd?

(171) The Borsa family, bankers from Venice, established the first stock exchange in the world in 1460 in the town of Bruges. Shortly after arriving, the Borsas changed their name to der Bourse. In which European country did they establish this stock exchange?

(172) The purchase or sale of securities in quantities of fewer than the standard trading lot—100 shares of stock or $1,000 worth of bonds—is referred to by what name?

(173) Compiled by the Conference Board, this monthly composite of ten economic measurements is used to track and help forecast changing patterns in the U.S. economy. Name this economic indicator.

(174) The SEC abolished fixed commissions over a seven year period. In what year were fixed commissions completely abolished?

(175) To be quoted via Pink Sheets, companies are required to fulfill what requirements?

(176) What is the largest single futures and options exchange in the United States?

(177) An order to buy or sell a security at a specific price rather than buying or selling at the current market price is referred to by what name?

(178) How many actual bells (not rings) are rung to signal the opening and closing of trading on the NYSE?

(179) How many companies are included in the Dow Jones Industrial Average?

(180) The New York Stock Exchange adopted its current name in 1863. What was the previous name?

(181) The first stock index was created in 1884 by Charles Dow. Name the index.

(182) This act of Congress is known as the "Public Company Accounting Reform and Investor Protection Act" in the U.S. Senate and the "Corporate and Auditing Accountability and Responsibility Act" in the U.S. House. What is its more common name?

(183) How many seats are there on the NYSE?

(184) True or False: Stock splits themselves mean you made money.

(185) What did the Buttonwood Agreement essentially establish?

(186) What is the name for an offer to acquire the shares of a corporation, typically with the intent to takeover the targeted corporation?

(187) An order to sell if a security falls to a certain price is called what?

(188) Domino's Pizza, Little Caesars, and Hungry Howie's (private) are all headquartered in which U.S. metropolitan area?

(189) How many user access levels exist with NASDAQ quotes?

(190) In 1976, specialists began handling what type of lots in their stocks?

(191) This agreement, becoming effective January 1, 1994, was signed by the governments of Canada, Mexico, and the United States to create a trilateral trade bloc in North America. Name this agreement.

(192) What does "GTC" stand for in regards to the time element of stock orders?

(193) What does the Case–Shiller index track?

(194) What does CFTC stand for?

(195)   What is the largest stock exchange in Europe as measured by market capitalization?

(196)   Approximately how much higher was the Dow Jones Industrial Average at the beginning of the United States entry into World War II to the end of the war?

(197)   What "street" is considered Canada's Wall Street?

(198)   In 1973, two Canadian stock exchanges merged to form the Montreal Stock Exchange. Name the two exchanges.

(199)   On January 26, 2000, an altercation during filming of the music video for "Sleep Now in the Fire", which was directed by Michael Moore, caused the doors of the NYSE to be closed. Which rock band was escorted from the site by security?

(200)   In what year did the Dow Jones Industrial Average first close over 1,000? (a) 1928, (b) 1947, (c) 1959, (d) 1968, (e) 1972

(201)   What is the name for when a stock is removed from trading on a stock exchange?

(202)   What does CPI stand for?

(203)   In 1900, manufacturing overtook agriculture and what other industry as the main attraction on Wall Street? *Railroads*

(204)   What gold coin supplanted the Krugerrand as the world's most popular gold coin?

(205) What is the real name for "Obamacare"?

(206) As of 2013, how many stocks are included in the Wilshire 5000 Index?

(207) In the year 2000, about 20 percent of all jobs in America were manufacturing jobs. About what percent of all jobs in America today are considered manufacturing jobs?

(208) In what year did the Dow Jones Industrial Average first close over 10,000?

(209) In what year did the New York Stock Exchange record its highest single day of trading volume at 7,341,505,961 shares?

(210) The All Ordinaries, or All Ords, is an index of which stock exchange?

(211) What does DJIA stand for?

(212) What index does the QQQ ETF track?

(213) What is the Japanese index equivalent of the Dow Jones Industrial Average?

(214) What does CBOT stand for?

(215) For how many years were fixed commission rates in place by law until completely phased out in 1975?

# CHAPTER 3

# STOCKS, COMPANIES, AND ORGANIZATIONS
*Inside What Makes Wall Street Tick*

**"** *It's a bad bargain where nobody gains.* **"**

- ENGLISH PROVERB

**"** *The first man gets the oyster, the second man gets the shell.* **"**

- ANDREW CARNEGIE

(216) What is the highest priced stock listed on the New York Stock Exchange as of 2013?

(217) Boone Pickens and Carl Icahn attempted independent hostile takeovers of what company that was ultimately successful in fighting off both attempts?

(218) Founded in 1889 and based in Omaha, Nebraska, this publicly owned investment manager primarily engages in the insurance and reinsurance of property and casualty risks businesses. Name this company run by Warren Buffet.

(219) Ginnie Mae is an acronym for what?

(220) Headquartered at the Philadelphia Navy Yard, this S&P 500 constituent company originated as "The Free People's Store" in 1970 focusing on "funky" fashion and household products. Name this company.

(221) Located in San Francisco, this insurance company is housed in a building where the top is shaped like a pyramid. Name this company.

(222) Name the first U.S. corporation to report earnings of more than $1 billion.

(223) Name the independent self-regulatory organization and watchdog of the commodities and futures industry in the United States.

(224) The Discover Card, launched in 1985, was originally issued by what company?

(225) This company was established in 1891 as the United States subsidiary of a German company with a near identical name. Name this company confiscated by the U.S. government during World War I and subsequently established as an independent American company.

(226) This company was founded in 1911 as the Computing Tabulating Recording Corporation through a merger of three companies: the Tabulating Machine Company, the International Time Recording Company, and the Computing Scale Corporation. Name this company that adopted its current name in 1924.

(227) This company, one of the world's largest offshore drilling contractors, owns nearly half of the 50 or so deepwater platforms in the world. Name this company.

(228) This company, the owner of Warner Brothers and HBO, is the world's second largest entertainment conglomerate in terms of revenue (behind Disney). Name this company.

(229) This S&P 500 constituent company is recognized as the largest retailer of wine in the world. Name this company.

(230) What was the first financial institution to hold assets physically on Wall Street?

(231) What international financial institution had its beginnings at a 1944 conference at Bretton Woods in the state of New Hampshire?

(232) What is the full legal name for energy company Shell?

(233) What is the legal name for the company commonly known as Sallie Mae but originally named the Student Loan Marketing Association?

(234) What is the name for the central banking system of the United States?

(235) Where is the Federal Reserve headquartered?

(236) Which of the big three automobile companies has never declared bankruptcy—Chrysler, Ford, or General Motors?

(237) Which oil and natural gas exploration and production company began in 1887 as The Ohio Oil Company?

(238) What is the official mascot of The Walt Disney Company?

(239) Who is the world's largest broadline food distributor?

(240) According to *Forbes* magazine, which U.S. private or public company is the largest employer in the world with 2.2 million global employees as of March 31, 2012?

(241) Based in Seattle, Washington, this company is the largest coffeehouse company in the world with more than 17,000 stores in 55 countries. Name this company.

(242) Employing over 113,000 people of more than 140 nationalities working in approximately 85 countries, this company is the world's largest oilfield services company. Name this company.

(243) Founded in 1898, Goodyear Tire & Rubber has one of the most recognizable advertising icons in America. What is this icon? (Hint: College Football)

(244) Headquartered in Clayton, Missouri, this privately held company owns Enterprise Rent-A-Car, National Car Rental, Alamo Rent A Car, WeCar and a commercial fleet. Name this company.

(245) Name John D. Rockefeller's first national corporation.

(246) This company, acquired by rival Adobe Systems in 2005, was a graphics and web development software company that produced such products as Flash and Dreamweaver. Name this company.

(247) The stock of what company trades under the ticker symbol "JACK"?

(248) Name the largest share registry company in the world.

(249) This company, the inventor of the laser printer in 1969, was founded in 1906 as The Haloid Photographic Company and originally manufactured photographic paper and equipment. Name this company.

(250) Name the corporation created by the reorganization of the Maxwell Motor Company.

(251) This company, originally known as Ask Jeeves, is a question-answering focused web search engine founded in 1996 and acquired in 2005 by InterActiveCorp for about $1.85 billion. Name this company.

(252) Name the largest credit union in the United States as ranked by assets and membership as of 2013.

(253) This global e-commerce company, now owned by eBay, was formed though the merger of Confinity and X.com in March 2000. Name this company.

(254) This S&P 500 constituent company is the largest auto retailer in the United States and was founded in 1996 by entrepreneur H. Wayne Huizenga who also founded Blockbuster and Waste Management. Name this company.

(255) What does IMF, the international financial institution established in 1944, stand for?

(256) What is the name for an electronic registration of ownership of a stock or bond?

(257) What is the name for the paper document representing ownership of a security?

(258) What is the ticker symbol for Southwest Airlines?

(259) What parent company owns Olive Garden, LongHorn Steakhouse, and Red Lobster?

(260) Which company owns the CBOT, NYMEX, and COMEX?

(261) Which one of the following brewing companies is owned by a foreign company? (a) Anheuser-Busch Companies, (b) Coors Brewing Company, (c) Miller Brewing Company

(262) Which publicly-traded corporation traded under the ticker symbol "C" before Citibank began using it?

(263) Who is known for "The Fastest Way to Send Money" tag line?

(264) Allure of The Seas and Oasis of The Seas are by far the largest cruise ships in the world as measured by gross tonnage. Which publicly-traded company owns and operates these two mammoth ships?

(265) At which restaurant chain are cups and burger wrappings marked with Bible citations?

(266) During the 1950s, Sears and Roebuck marketed automobiles under what brand name?

(267) Formerly known as the National Biscuit Company, this company now owned by Kraft operates the world's largest bakery out of Chicago. Name this company.

(268) Founded in 1926, this airline company approved a merger with Delta in 2008. Name this airline.

(269) Headquartered in Memphis, Tennessee, this company is the largest pulp and paper company in the world. Name this company with approximately 59,500 employees.

(270) Which parent company owns and operates the University of Phoenix, Western International University, and the College for Financial Planning?

(271) What was the first U.S. corporation to be worth more than $1 billion in assets?

(272) Name the investment firm co-founded by J.P. Morgan's grandson Harry.

(273) The stock of what company trades under the ticker symbol "FUN"?

(274) The stock of what company trades under the ticker symbol "MO"?

(275) This company's subsidiaries include KraftMaid Cabinetry, Merillat, and Delta Faucet Company. Name this company that went public on the Detroit Stock Exchange in 1936.

(276) This Dallas-based bank was founded in Detroit and purchased the naming rights to the Detroit Tigers baseball stadium before relocating to Texas. Name this bank.

(277) This foreign bank, the first bank from its country to list on the NYSE (in October 2001), employs over 11,000 employees in 28 states and 90 cities across the United States. Name this bank.

(278) Which company operates the restaurants Chili's Grill & Bar and Maggiano's Little Italy and trades under the ticker symbol "EAT"?

(279) Which organization issues all exchange-listed securities options in the United States and guarantees all transactions in those options?

(280) This mega industrial corporation was founded by William "Billy" Durant. Name this corporation.

(281) What is the name given to financial services corporations created by the United States Congress to enhance the flow of credit and improve efficiency and transparences?

(282) What is the ticker symbol for United States Steel Corporation?

(283) What was the largest physical size for a bond certificate on one piece of paper?

(284) Which company has higher annual revenues—IBM, Intel, or Microsoft?

(285) Which corporation trades under the single letter ticker symbol "S"?

(286) This suburban Minneapolis, Minnesota-based company is the world's largest medical technology company. Name this company that trades under the "MDT" ticker symbol.

(287) Founded in 1887, this St. Louis, Missouri-based brokerage firm was acquired in 2007 by Wachovia Bank, itself acquired by Wells Fargo soon thereafter. Name the firm.

(288) Based in Nashville, Tennessee, this company is the largest private operator of health care facilities in the world. Name this company with about 180,000 global employees.

(289) Drexel, Morgan & Co. was the first company established by which investment titan?

(290) Founded in 1886 and headquartered in Atlanta, this publicly-traded company manufactures, distributes, and markets nonalcoholic beverage concentrates and syrups worldwide. Name this company that owns Sprite and Fanta.

(291) Founded in 1944, this Washington, DC-based international organization oversees the global financial system by following the macroeconomic policies of its member countries. Name this organization.

(292) Founded in 1989, this company is North America's largest provider of medical waste services specializing in collecting and disposing medical waste, recalled and expired medical products, and infection control management and services. Name this company.

(293) How many alphanumeric characters comprise a CUSIP?

(294) According to Diversity, Inc., which U.S. company is the top company for diversity in the office as of 2012?

(295) Published papers listing the prices for municipal bonds were formerly printed on what color paper?

(296) The stock of what company trades under the ticker symbol "FOOT"?

(297) This bank is remembered as the largest bank failure in American financial history. Prior to the receivership action, it was the sixth-largest bank in the United States with over $325 billion in assets. Name this bank.

(298) What was the previous derivation name for Apple, Inc.?

(299) The stock of what company trades under the ticker symbol "HOT"?

(300) This dually stock listed British company is the world's largest producer of spirits with such brands as Smirnoff, Johnnie Walker, Baileys, and Guinness. Name this company.

(301) This company's name is derived from the made-up Greek word "xerography," dubbed "dry writing." Name this company.

(302) This Indianapolis-based company is the largest real estate investment trust in the United States. Name this S&P 500 constituent company.

(303) This Michigan-based company is one of the largest homebuilders in the country. Name this company whose motto is "Homeowner for Life."

(304) True/False: The Federal Reserve has its own law enforcement arm called the Federal Reserve Police.

(305) What is the largest pulp and paper company in the world with approximately 60,000 employees and headquartered in Memphis, Tennessee?

(306) What was the first company listed on the NYSE—a stock even President George Washington theoretically could have purchased?

(307) Which farm and construction equipment company— among other business endeavors—was founded in 1837 and is based in Moline, Illinois?

(308) Which American company is the largest builder of naval vessels in the world?

(309) Which company initially began as "Jerry's guide to the world wide web"?

(310) Which report—published eight times a year—is described as a collection of "anecdotal information on current economic conditions" by each Federal Reserve Bank in its district from "bank and branch directors and interviews with key business contacts, economists, market experts, and others."?

(311) Who is the largest drug retailing chain in the United States with approximately 8,300 locations across all 50 states, the District of Columbia, and Puerto Rico?

(312) According to the Audit Bureau of Circulation, which publication has the largest circulation among newspapers in the United States?

(313) Esso was the former name for what mega-American publicly-traded corporation?

(314) FINRA is the successor to which self-regulatory organization?

(315) Founded in 1906, this Battle Creek, Michigan company was the first to offer premiums (i.e. toys) in its cereal boxes and first to fortify its cereals. Name this company.

(316) Goodrich Corporation was originally called B.F. Goodrich. What did the letters "B" and "F" stand for?

(317) How many employees of Microsoft have become billionaires and millionaires from their holdings of Microsoft stock?

(318) How was Xerox spelled prior to its current form?

(319) The U.S. government forced what major American company to divest on January 1, 1984?

(320) The stock of what company trades under the ticker symbol "HIT"?

(321) This Alexandria, Virginia-based private multimedia financial-services company was founded in July 1993 with its name taken from Shakespeare's "As You Like It." Name this company.

(322) The stock of what company trades under the ticker symbol "SAM"?

(323) This Boston-based mutual fund company was founded in 1946, employs close to 40,000 people worldwide, and manages approximately $1.5 trillion in assets. Name this company where the family of the founder still owns close to half of the company.

(324) This supermarket chain is based in Austin, Texas, and emphasizes "natural and organic products." Name this company ranked among the most socially-responsible businesses in the United States.

(325) This Nevada-based and S&P 500 constituent company manufactures roughly half of the slot machines in the United States. Name this company.

(326) This Mountain View, California, company is the largest maker of security software for computers and best known for its Norton brand. Name this member company of the S&P 500 index.

(327) This organization, a non-profit federal corporation under the jurisdiction of the Department of Labor, protects retirement incomes of 44 million American workers in over 30,000 private-sector defined pension plans. Name this organization.

(328) What are the three most prominent credit rating agencies?

(329) What is the name for the price at which a security can be sold when placing a market order?

(330) Which major brokerage firm is headquartered in Tampa, Florida?

(331) Which brokerage firm—today part of a larger brokerage firm—was founded in 1924 by brothers with the first names of Jean, Guy, John, and Dean?

(332) As of 2013, this company has held the record for most patents generated by a company for 20 consecutive years. Name this company whose employees have garnered five Nobel Prizes.

(333) Which company owns the golf brands Titleist, FootJoy, and Pinnacle Golf?

(334) Which media conglomerate owns BET Networks, MTV Networks, and Paramount Pictures?

(335) Which S&P 500 constituent company trades under the ticker symbol "BIG"?

(336) "Where's the beef?" is a catchphrase from a popular 1984 commercial from what company?

(337) According to the Fortune Global 500, this company is the world's largest mutual "P&C" (property & casualty insurance) firm. Name this company.

(338) FDIC protects bank customers while credit union customers are protected by what?

(339) For which broad asset class or investment security is PIMCO most known?

(340) Founded in 1948, this company is the world's first and largest accounting and finance staffing firm with over 400 locations worldwide. Name this company.

(341) Headquartered in Seattle, Washington, this company is the largest online retailer in the United States with nearly three times the Internet sales revenue of the runner up. Name this company.

(342) How many years is a full-term for a Federal Reserve governor?

(343) The stock of what company trades under the ticker symbol "CASH"?

(344) In 1903, Senator James Couzens purchased $2,500 worth of what stock that he sold for $30 million twelve years later in 1915?

(345) This auto and truck parts company was founded in 1885 by Professor Warren S. Johnson, inventor of the first electric room thermostat. Name this company with approximately 162,000 employees worldwide.

(346) The stock of what company trades under the ticker symbol "TOY"?

(347) This Cambridge, Massachusetts-based defense contractor is the world's largest producer of guided missiles. Name this company.

(348) This company is the largest maker of hand tools, power tools, and related accessories in the United State. Name this company with an impressive 40% market share in tools.

(349) Founded under the name Bank of Italy by Italian immigrant Amadeo Giannini, this bank was once the largest commercial bank in the world. What is the modern name for this bank?

(350) This parent company owns and operates Old Navy, Banana Republic, Piperlime, and Athleta brand names. Name this company founded in 1969 and based in San Francisco, California.

(351) This S&P 500 constituent company boasts the jean brands Wrangler, Lee Jeans, Rustler, and Chic. Name this company that also owns the brand Nautica.

(352) United States monetary policy is set by which entity?

(353) What is the ticker symbol for NASDAQ OMX Group?

(354) What does the abbreviation KKR, the buyout firm, stand for?

(355) Which company owns the largest railroad network with over 32,000 miles in the United States?

(356) Which company ran the "Blue Light Special"?

(357) Which company, based in Beaverton, Oregon, is the world's leading supplier of athletic shoes and apparel as well as a major manufacturer of sports equipment?

(358) Which computer maker is based in Round Rock, a suburb of Austin, Texas?

(359) Which mega-corporation acquired Kidder, Peabody & Co. in 1981?

(360) Which two waste management companies handle more than half of all garbage collection in the United States?

(361) Advanced Micro Devices is the only significant rival to which computer processor developer and manufacturer?

(362) Boeing Transport and National Air Transport merged to create what company in 1930?

(363) Fill in the blanks: Credit Suisse F_____ B_____

(364) Founded in 1775, this company became the oldest company to list on the New York Stock Exchange when it joined in 1999. Name this company acquired by RR Donnelley in 2010.

(365) Founded in 1983 and listed on the NASDAQ, this company makes the personal finance programs Quicken and TurboTax as well as the small business accounting program QuickBooks. Name this company.

(366) How many District Reserve Banks comprise the Federal Reserve?

(367) In 1997, this National Football League team became the NFL's only publicly held (but not exchange traded) team. Name the team.

(368) In what decade did the Ford Motor Company go public?

(369) The stock of what company trades under the ticker symbol "FAST"?

(370) This brokerage firm, known for its one person offices, is listed in the top ten best companies to work for in America by CNNMoney. Name this company.

(371) This Chicago-based company is most widely known for its expertise with asset allocation research and modeling. Name this company.

(372) What food was developed by Whirlpool Corporation under contract to NASA for the Apollo missions?

(373) This company is the largest retailer of decorative home furnishings and gifts in North America. Who is it?

(374) This Orrville, Ohio company was started in 1872 with its first product being apple butter. Name this company.

(375) United States Steel Corporation was renamed in 1991, but reverted back to its current name in 2001. By what name was it known as during that 10-year period?

(376) What "committee" of the Federal Reserve Board buys and sells United States Treasury securities?

(377) What do Cargill and Koch Industries have in common?

(378) What does the acronym OWS stand for having become popular in 2011?

(379) What is the ticker symbol for National Beverage Corp., owner of brands Faygo, Shasta, Everfresh, and La Croix Sparkling Water among others?

(380) Which company was founded in January 1994 and incorporated the following year by Jerry Yang and David Filo?

(381) Which corporation trades under the single letter ticker symbol "A"?

(382) Which international news agency—established in 1851 and headquartered in London—was acquired by The Thomson Corporation in 2008 and subsequently renamed?

(383) Which corporation trades under the single letter ticker symbol "B"? (a) Boeing, (b) Barnes Group, (c) Barnes & Noble, (d) Becton Properties

(384) Which San Francisco company enables its users to send and read text-based posts of up to 140 characters?

(385) Which U.S. corporation was once known by the name Computer-Tabulator-Recorder Company?

(386) As of 2011, who is the largest airline in the United States based on scheduled passengers carried?

(387) Caught up in an accounting fraud that led to the ouster of CEO Bernard Ebbers and other executives, this company went bankrupt and was ultimately acquired by Verizon for $7.6 billion in 2005. Name this company.

(388) Founded as a textile remnant company under the name Hassenfeld Brothers, this company's first toy hit was Mr. Potato Head. Name this company.

(389) Founded in 1870, this company engages in the exploration, production, transportation, and sale of crude oil and natural gas. Name this company that moved its headquarters from New York to the Las Colinas area of Irving, Texas in 1989.

(390) Freddie Mae is an acronym for what?

(391) J.P. Morgan established what oil company the year of the 1929 crash?

(392) In 2006, Yahoo offered to buy this company for $1.4 billion but discussions broke down by July of the same year. Name this company now valued substantially more than the $1.4 billion offer price.

(393) This Chicago-based company is known for its star ranking system for mutual funds and style and size box category system. Name this company.

(394) MasterCard was originally known by what other similar name?

(395) This Cincinnati-based company is the country's largest grocery store chain and its second-largest grocery retailer by volume. Name this company.

(396) This company is the largest cable operator, home Internet service provider, and fourth largest home telephone service provider in the United States. Name this company.

(397) This company is the largest U.S. newspaper publisher as measured by total daily circulation of all newspapers combined that it publishes. Name this company.

(398) This company was founded in 1995 under the name AuctionWeb in San Jose by French-born Iranian-American computer programmer Pierre Omidyar. Name this company.

(399) This S&P 500 and Dow Jones component company is the largest exporter by value in the United States. Name this company that relocated its corporate headquarters to Chicago in 2001.

(400) What did the letters in the company name "CVS" originally stand for?

(401) What do the letters "Q" & "E" stand for in regards to the Fed's QE2?

(402) What does the word "Chipotle," as in Chipotle Mexican Grill, mean in Spanish?

(403) What does NYMEX stand for?

(404) What stock holds the record for the highest face value at $500,000?

(405) Which energy company trades under the ticker symbol "BTU"?

(406) Headquartered in Charlotte, North Carolina, this company is the largest electric power holding company in the United States. Name the company.

(407) Which investment firm—now part of Morgan Stanley—advertised itself as making money the old-fashioned way, "we earn it"?

(408) Which investment management firm owns the iShares family of ETFs?

(409) At its peak in the 1950s and 1960s, this now-acquired company employed one million people with roughly $300 billion in revenues based on 2006 dollars. Name this company, now a subsidiary of its parent company who took its name.

(410) Which two companies are the top two largest defense contractors in the United States?

(411) Who is the largest pharmaceuticals company in the world with sales of $122 billion in fiscal year 2012?

(412) This company is the largest non-hazardous solid waste management company in the United States. Name this company.

(413) Founded in 1917, this publicly-traded corporation with headquarters in Rockefeller Center is the parent company of Standard & Poor's, Platts, and J.D. Power and Associates. Name this company.

(414) Founded in Minneapolis in 1902 as the Dayton Dry Goods Company, this company is the second-largest discount retailer in the United States trailing only Walmart. Name this Fortune 500 company.

(415) Headquartered in Thousand Oaks, California, this company is the world's largest independent biotechnology firm. Name this company.

(416) In 2007, the stock of Bear Stearns was trading near $170 per share. For what price did J.P. Morgan Chase purchase the company one year later during the financial crisis?

(417) This company was founded as the New York Gas Light Company and holds the record as the longest listed company on the New York Stock Exchange. What is the modern name for this company?

(418) Name the first publicly-traded security in the United States.

(419) This company began in 1985 as Long Distance Discount Services (LDDS). Name this company that went public in 1989 through the merger with Advantage Companies.

(420) Which financial entity holds more than $100 billion worth of gold in vaults located 80 feet below street level in New York City?

(421) This company operates approximately 37,000 restaurants in 110 countries and territories under the KFC, Pizza Hut, Taco Bell, Long John Silver's, and A&W All-American Food Restaurants brands. Name this company.

(422) This company was the largest privately-owned shipyard in the United States prior to being purchased by Northrop Grumman in 2001. Name this company that produced the largest aircraft carrier in the world to date.

(423) This company, established by a pharmacist who was also a veteran of the American Civil War, was the first pharmaceutical company to mass-produce penicillin. Name this Indianapolis-based Fortune 500 company whose product line includes Prozac and Humalog.

(424) This company, founded in California in 1925 and now headquartered in Illinois, is the world's largest manufacturer of construction and mining equipment, diesel and natural gas engines, and industrial gas turbines. Name this company.

(425) To ensure that this government entity remains non-partisan, no more than three out of a total of five commissioners may belong to the same political party. Name this entity.

(426) What does AT&T stand for?

(427) What do Global Crossing, Nabors Industries, and Seagate Technology have in common?

(428) What economic organization was established in 1957 in Rome, Italy?

(429) What does OPEC stand for?

(430) What was the former name for KB Homes, which changed its name in 2001?

(431) Which indirect entity of the United States government issues the only mortgage-backed securities backed by the full faith and credit guaranty of the United States government?

(432) Which mega-corporation is often referred to as "Big Blue"?

(433) Which oilfield services corporation founded in Duncan, Oklahoma, is forever linked to former U.S. Vice President Dick Cheney?

(434) Who are the three largest consumer credit reporting agencies in the United States?

(435) Who is the largest manufacturer of private label over-the-counter pharmaceuticals in the United States?

(436) At the end of 2010, this restaurant surpassed McDonald's with the most locations worldwide. Name this privately-held restaurant chain owned by Doctor's Associates.

(437) Founded in 1873, this company is a diversified, British-Australian, multinational mining and resources group with headquarters in London and Melbourne. Name this company.

(438) FPL, now a subsidiary of NextEra Energy and based in Juno Beach, Florida, is the third largest utility company in the United States. What does FPL stand for?

(439) Who is the world's largest toy company based on revenue?

(440) In terms of total revenue, this Georgia-based company is the largest home improvement retailer in the United States and fourth largest general retailer. Name this company.

(441) In what year was the United States Federal Reserve established?

(442) Name the British–American company ranked as the world's largest cruise ship operator.

(443) This company is North America's largest owner and operator of wind and solar electricity generating assets. Name this company.

(444) This company, now a subsidiary of Disney, was founded in 1996 by stay-at-home mom and former teacher Julie Aigner-Clark at her home in suburban Alpharetta, Georgia. Name this company known for its Baby Mozart (1998), Baby Bach (1999), and other "Baby" videos.

(445) This company is the largest private landowner in the United States. Name this company.

(446) What was the ticker symbol for Hewlett-Packard prior to its acquisition of Compaq?

(447) This company operates the second largest civil aircraft fleet in the world—but does not carry passengers for the bulk of its business. Name this company.

(448) This company, headquartered in Los Angeles, is the world's largest commercial real estate services firm in terms of 2012 revenue. Name this company with approximately 34,000 employees.

(449) This company, one of the first web-based email services, was launched in July 1996 and acquired by Microsoft in 1997 for an estimated $400 million. Name this company.

(450) UPS is a package delivery company headquartered in Sandy Springs, Georgia. What does the acronym UPS stand for?

(451) What does the word "CUSIP" stand for?

(452) During the period of 1989 to 2010, which company gave the most in political campaign contributions?

(453) What is the name for state securities laws?

(454) What does ERISA stand for?

(455) Which major discount brokerage firm is based in San Francisco?

(456) Which NYSE member firm became the first to be listed on the NYSE exchange?

(457) Who conducts open-market operations?

(458) Which state agency manages the largest public pension fund in the United States?

(459) Halliburton, one of the world's largest oilfield services company, has dual headquarters located in Houston and what international city?

# CHAPTER 4

# PRODUCTS, LOGOS, SLOGANS, AND NAMES
## All About Corporate Identity

*" My idea of a group decision is to look in the mirror. "*

**- WARREN BUFFETT**

*" Good management consists in showing average people how to do the work of superior people. "*

**- JOHN D. ROCKEFELLER**

(460) Finish this classic slogan from FedEx: "When it absolutely, _____ has to be there overnight"

(461) Finish this company slogan: "Nothing Runs Like a _____"

(462) The slogan for which product from parent company Kraft Foods is "Good to the Last Drop"?

(463) Which company uses the slogan "I'm Lovin' It"?

(464) Which company—established in 1869—used the slogan "Mmm Mmm Good" from 1978 to 2010?

(465) Who used the slogans "Join in" (2000), "We never stop working for you" (early 2000s), "Can you hear me now? Good" (mid-2000s), and "Rule the Air" (2010)?

(466) According to most people, what consumer product is considered the biggest flop of all time?

(467) If you look closely, what symbol is incorporated into the FedEx logo?

(468) This Columbus, Ohio, headquartered restaurant chain has the slogan "Down on the Farm." Name this company.

(469) This company, known for using the head of a duck in its logo, is the largest provider of supplemental insurance in the United States. Name this company.

(470) Which company uses the slogan "You're in Good Hands"?

(471) Which telecommunications company introduced the RAZR (pronounced as "razor") mobile phone?

(472) Finish this company slogan: "Like a good _____, State Farm is there."

(473) Jif, Crisco, Pillsbury, Hungry Jack, and Martha White are the product brands of what Orrville, Ohio-based company?

(474) This cereal from General Mills is known as "The Breakfast of Champions." Name the cereal.

(475) What is the primary color of both the Goldman Sachs and American Express corporate logos?

(476) Which company uses the slogan "That was Easy"?

(477) Who is "The Document Company"?

(478) Ben & Jerry's was originally supposed to sell what product before changing to ice cream?

(479) Finish this GEICO slogan: "15 Minutes Could Save You _____ on Car Insurance."

(480) Nike's logo was created in 1971 by graphics design student Carolyn Davidson while enrolled at Portland State University for a mere $35. What is the logo called?

(481) What did the letters in the company name AOL originally stand for?

(482) Fill in the blank: "When _____ talks, people listen."

(483) Which Philadelphia-based petroleum and petrochemical manufacturer uses a logo with a red piercing arrow?

(484) Which investment firm features a lion in its logo and advertisements?

(485) The 1982 smash hit *E.T. the Extra-Terrestrial* originally planned to feature M&Ms in the movie but switched when the Mars company declined the invitation. What back-up product did the movie feature instead?

(486) This company designs and manufactures clothing and accessories, primarily watches and jewelry. Who is this company whose name represents the nickname the founding brothers had for their father?

(487) What is the name of the personal assistant that accepts voice commands on Apple products?

(488) Which company uses the slogan "Don't Leave Home Without it"?

(489) Finish this company slogan: "There Are Some Things Money Can't Buy. For Everything Else, There's _____."

(490) The Newell Rubbermaid company markets a brand of correction fluid that was invented by Bette Nesmith Graham, the mother of Robert Michael Nesmith best known as a member of the musical group The Monkees. What did Bette invent?

(491) What consumer product was purchased for $18.5 million from the family of "Uncle Jack" in 1956?

(492) What is the trademark logo of Target Corporation?

(493) Which company uses the slogan "Have It Your Way"?

(494) Play-Doh was first manufactured in Cincinnati, Ohio, in the 1930s. What was its original purpose?

(495) This company's brand name products include Kleenex facial tissue, Cottonelle, Scott and Andrex toilet paper, and Huggies disposable diapers. Name this company.

(496) What was the first consumer product to have a bar code included on its wrapper?

(497) Which company uses the slogan "Just Do It"?

(498) Which iconic logo, first used in 1870, was briefly owned by Citigroup and now owned by Travelers, its original designer?

(499) The logo of this company, a subsidiary of VF Corporation, is an interpretation of Half Dome, a massive granitic monolith in Yosemite National Park. Name this company.

(500) What are the four words in the Harley-Davidson logo?

(501) The name for this network technology producer company, now a part of Hewlett-Packard, was derived from the names *com*puter, *com*munication, and *com*patibility. Name this company.

(502) Which company uses the slogan "We Bring Good Things to Life"?

(503) Which company uses the Rock of Gibraltar as its logo?

(504) Which product was recalled worldwide in 1994 by Intel due to the FDIV bug?

(505) What product is "Just what the Dr ordered"?

(506) Which company uses the slogan "Improving Home Improvement"?

(507) Which product from General Mills is associated with the slogan "Kid tested, mother approved"?

(508) Which two prominent bankers met in 1909 as roommates at the YMCA and later launched one of the leading brokerage firms in the country that even today uses their last names?

(509) Fill in the blank from this Capital One slogan: "What's in your _____?"

(510) The name of which company is derived from the words "group" and "coupon"?

(511) Which company is known for its marketing slogan "57 Varieties"?

(512) Which major U.S. company uses the image of a deer in its logo?

(513) Which corporation includes a large red letter "Z" in its name and logo?

(514) Who uses the slogan "First in Business Worldwide"?

# CHAPTER 5

# SECURITIES, STRATEGIES, AND TERMS

*Revealing How Wall Street
Wealth is Made*

*" Thinking is the hardest work there is, which is the
probable reason why so few engage in it. "*

– HENRY FORD

*" Stocks are bought on expectations, not facts. "*

– GERALD M. LOEB

(515) As of 2013, what is the largest exchange-traded fund as ranked by assets under management?

(516) If a corporation were to go bankrupt, do common shareholders, preferred shareholders, or bondholders have first rights to the assets?

(517) MSCI market indexes are widely followed and highly popular. What does MSCI stand for?

(518) This investment term is defined as a small document representing an interest payment that is cut from a bond and cashed in or deposited. What is this term?

(519) U.S. Treasury bills are sold weekly by competitive auction to institutional investors. What are the two terms of maturity (in weeks) sold at auction?

(520) A bond that was originally issued below its face or par value is called what?

(521) What does the slang expression "Peruvian bond" refer to?

(522) What is the name for large-denomination bank certificates of deposit with balances of at least $100,000 and sometimes $1 million or more?

(523) What is the name for municipal bonds issued to finance public projects, such as airports and roadways?

(524) Forwards, futures, options, warrants, and swaps are all common contract types of what broad category of investment?

(525) What U.S. government bond purchased at a discount are used to pay off estate taxes at full face value?

(526) What U.S. government issued bond has a maturity of between one and ten years?

(527) Which index does the ETF nicknamed "Diamonds" track?

(528) If market interest rates decline rapidly, what is the general effect on the market prices for bonds?

(529) "Qubes" is the nickname for an ETF that tracks which index?

(530) Treasury inflation-protected securities, or TIPs, are linked to which index?

(531) What does ADR, an investible security, stand for?

(532) What is another name for when an employee stock option is out-of-the-money and currently worthless?

(533) What is the name for a type of short-term negotiable debt instrument issued by a non-financial corporation but guaranteed as to principal and interest by the issuing entity's bank?

(534) What is the name for the date on which a bond or preferred stock can be redeemed by the issuer prior to maturity?

(535) Mutual funds with a fixed number of shares (or units) are better known as what?

(536) When a company divests one of its existing subsidiaries or divisions to form a separate company, this is commonly called what?

(537) Which category of company typically pays the higher dividend yield—growth companies or value companies?

(538) If someone were to mention the name Long-term Equity AnticiPation Securities, or LEAPS, what general type of investment are they referring to?

(539) A bond issued by a state, county, or city is called by what name?

(540) If a company decides to reduce its number of existing common stock shares and increase its stock price by consolidating the shares in a 1-for-2 split, what is this called?

(541) Income paid on a bond is called what?

(542) The number of shares available to the public for trading purposes is referred to by what name?

(543) U.S. Treasury bills have maturities of less than what time period?

(544) When an investor writes, or sells, a call option but does not own the underlying security (e.g. stock, ETF), the option is described as what?

(545) What is the name for a bond or other debt security that is guaranteed by the issuer by pledging, or assigning, collateral to investors?

(546) What is the name for an unsecured bond that is backed only by the full faith and credit of an issuer?

(547) What is the name for the list of option contracts for a single underlying instrument?

(548) What types of ETFs are Direxion and ProShares known for providing?

(549) What does ETF stand for?

(550) Which mutual fund share "Class" is associated with large upfront commissions?

(551) Most mutual funds are best described as what? (a) open-end funds, (b) closed-end funds, (c) exchange-traded funds, or (d) unit investment trusts?

(552) Investing specific dollar amounts on a regular basis to average out the cost of investments over time is referred to as what?

(553) STRIPS are associated with which type of fixed-income security?

(554) Weak, semistrong, and strong are three forms of which hypothesis promulgated by Professor Eugene Fama?

(555) What does LIBOR stand for?

(556) What does the symbol "€" represent?

(557) If you hear someone talking about "Forex," to what are they referring?

(558) What is the name for common stock that was outstanding in the market but was repurchased by the issuing company?

(559) What is the name for stocks trading at prices under $1?

(560) What is the name for the phenomenon whereby a rapid increase in the price of a stock occurs due to a lack of supply and an excess of demand for the stock?

(561) Which classification of light sweet crude oil is used to price two-thirds of the world's internationally traded crude oil supplies?

(562) Which investing strategy or approach encourages corporate practices that promote environmental stewardship, consumer protection, human rights, diversity, and avoids many businesses involved in alcohol, tobacco, and gambling?

(563) Which type of preferred stock is more common: Noncumulative (straight) preferred or cumulative preferred?

(564) Brent and West Texas Intermediate refer to what?

(565) Dividing current assets by current liabilities provides what statistical measure?

(566) Stock that is registered in a broker-dealer's name rather than in the name of the actual, or beneficial, owner is called what?

(567) What does EPS stand for?

(568) The "creation and redemption" mechanism/process is associated with what type of security?

(569) What does the acronym "MSRB" stand for?

(570) What is the benchmark instrument for determining the risk-free rate of return?

(571) What is the name of the interest rate charged to commercial banks and other depository institutions on loans they receive from their regional Federal Reserve Bank's lending facility?

(572) What is the name of the process when you transfer money from your 401k to your IRA?

(573) What is the term used to describe the total number of shares of a particular stock that investors have sold short?

(574) Which investment strategy, popularized by Michael B. O'Higgins, calls for annually investing in the ten highest dividend yielding stocks in the Dow Jones Industrial Average?

(575) Which of the following securities typically offers a higher dividend yield: common stock, convertible preferred stock, or nonconvertible preferred stock?

(576) A demand by a broker that an investor deposit further cash or securities to cover possible losses is called what?

(577) Contango is a pricing issue associated with which type of investments?

(578) Which term is used to describe a payout made to shareholders representing their share of a corporation's profit?

(579) The date on which a bond pays back its face or par value is called what?

(580) Is the total market capitalization bigger for common stock or preferred stock?

(581) What does REIT stand for?

(582) What does the acronym EBITDA stand for?

(583) What is the maximum number of days to maturity for commercial paper?

(584) What is the term used to explain an economic environment where inflation is negative—meaning falling prices?

(585) What term is used to describe a company's intangible value of its reputation, its satisfied clients, and its productive work force?

(586) Which type of equity security nearly always grants shareholder voting rights—preferred stock or common stock?

(587) What theory asserts that price movements do not follow any patterns or trends and that past price movements cannot be used to predict future price movements?

(588) What is the name for the interest charged by a brokerage firm on a loan given to an investor to purchase securities using the borrowed money?

(589) Bonds are usually redeemed at par, or face value. What is the traditional dollar amount per corporate bond?

(590) Expressed as a percentage of net asset value and normally annualized, this statistical measure calculates the volume of shares traded during a particular period, as a total of all shares listed. What is this measure called?

(591) Investors have the option of purchasing one of two types of sugar futures contracts—sugar #11 and sugar #16. What is the major difference between the two types?

(592) The stated interest rate, which does not take inflation into consideration, is called what?

(593) The terms "in-the-money", "at-the-money", and "out-of-the-money" refer to what type of investment?

(594) What does the acronym "FOMC" stand for?

(595) What is the name for a bond that is selling for less than its face or par value?

(596) What investment strategy involves borrowing shares through a broker, selling them in the open market, and pledging the sale proceeds as collateral on the borrowed funds until the stock price drops and the shares are purchased and returned to the broker?

(597) Fill in the blank: An _____ is the smallest possible incremental increase in a security's price, which, for stocks, is one cent.

(598) What type of "values" do the Ave Maria family of mutual funds adhere to?

(599) What type of currency is represented by the symbol "¥"?

(600) Which energy commodity trades under the ticker symbol "HO"?

(601) Which U.S. government issued security has the longest maturity—bills, bonds, or notes?

(602) Bull spreads and bear spreads are associated with which type of security?

(603) Investors who believe that the general wisdom and thinking of the market is always wrong and therefore invest opposite of the general market are referred to by what name?

(604) What type of bonds are issued in dollars in the United States by overseas companies and governments?

(605) Variable annuities are offered by what type of financial companies?

(606) What does YTM stand for?

(607) What is the general name for the type of bond that is exempt from federal income taxes?

(608) What is the term used to explain a slowdown in the rate of increase (i.e. inflation) of prices for goods and services?

(609) What type of bonds are considered the property of whoever holds them since there is no record of ownership like registered bonds?

(610) What type of option would you buy if you want the right to sell a certain security within a predetermined time at a predetermined price?

(611) Which mutual fund share "Class" typically has the highest annual expense ratio?

(612) With options, what is another name for the expiration price?

(613) What does the investment acronym CMO stand for?

(614) Futures contracts trade on organized exchanges. How do forward contracts trade?

(615) This investment term is defined as a nine-character alphanumeric code that identifies any North American security for the purpose of facilitating clearing and settlement of trades. What is this term?

(616) Municipal bonds that are backed by the full faith and credit of an issuing entity rather than backed by a specific revenue stream are called by what name?

(617) What type of investment trades under the ticker symbol "GLD"?

(618) Ownership of a security held in the name of the broker-dealer instead of the name of the investor is referred to as what?

(619) What does FDIC stand for?

(620) What feature of some preferred stock issues gives the owner the right to force the issuer to buy the shares back at a pre-determined price?

(621) What is the name for an offering circular that is given to investors by companies looking to go public, among other reasons?

(622) Illegal excessive buying and selling of securities by a financial advisor in a client's account with the primary aim of generating commissions is known as what?

(623) Which "Series" of securities license is called the "general securities representative"?

(624) What is the name for a large holding or transaction of stock—typically 10,000 shares or more?

(625) A corporate IOU (unsecured promissory note) is better known by what name?

(626) From a tax perspective, there are two types of stock dividends—one called ordinary. What is the name of the other type?

(627) The principal value of which Treasury security is adjusted based on the Consumer Price Index (CPI)?

(628) How do you calculate a P/E ratio?

(629) Straddle and strangles are hedging strategies that involve buying or selling what type of security?

(630) U.S. dollars on deposit in European banks are referred to as what?

(631) What does the "VIX" measure?

(632) What is the name for a negotiable security issued by a corporation (usually together with a bond or preferred stock) that gives the holder the right to purchase a certain amount of common stock at a predetermined price? (Hint: not an option)

(633) What is the name for high-yield, speculative corporate bonds with low credit ratings?

(634) Thirty-year bonds referred to as "Long Bonds" are issued by whom?

(635) What type of option grants the buyer the right to purchase a security at a predetermined price before a predetermined date?

(636) Which ETF trades under the ticker symbol "JNK"?

# CHAPTER 6

# MONEY, INVESTING, AND TAXES

*Understanding What Motivates and Drives Wall Street*

*" You cannot help men permanently by doing for them what they could and should do for themselves. "*

– ABRAHAM LINCOLN

*" Gold is tested by fire, man by gold. "*

– CHINESE PROVERB

(637) In regards to currency, what do the British Virgin Islands, Ecuador, El Salvador, Panama, the Turks and Caicos Islands, and Zimbabwe all have in common?

(638) Once every quarter—on the third Friday of March, June, September, and December—stock options, stock index options, stock index futures contracts, and single stock futures expire on the same day in the United States. What is this day called?

(639) The Federal Deposit Insurance Corporation (FDIC) guarantees the safety of deposits in member banks on a per depositor per bank basis. How much money is guaranteed per depositor per bank as of 2013?

(640) The sale and repurchase of the same security within 30 days disallows the recognition of any capital loss. What is this rule called?

(641) These "terminals" provide financial software tools such as analytics and an equity trading platform, data services, and news to financial companies and organizations around the world. What are these terminals called?

(642) What type of investment strategy calls for establishing a pattern of rolling maturity dates for a portfolio of fixed-income investments?

(643) When an employee is entitled to the contributions her employer has made to her retirement plan—including matching and discretionary contributions—after a certain period of service with the employer, this is called what?

(644) When the demand for shares of an IPO is greater than the number of shares being issued, the IPO is said to be what?

(645) When the interest rate on short-term U.S. Treasury issues is higher than the rate on long-term Treasury bonds, the yield curve is said to be what?

(646) Which is the only measurement of the U.S. money supply not published by the Federal Reserve—M0, M1, M2, or M3?

(647) JAGNOTES primarily reports what type of analyst events?

(648) Referred to as FASB, this independent, self-regulatory board establishes and interprets generally accepted accounting principles (GAAP) that corporations must follow. Name this board.

(649) This type of risk results from unpredictable factors, such as poor management decisions, successful competitive products, or suddenly obsolete technologies that may affect the securities issued by a particular company or group of similar companies. What is this risk called?

(650) True/False: Fiscal years can be 52 weeks and some 53 weeks.

(651) Under federal law, if your credit card is stolen, up to what amount of any fraudulent charges are you financially responsible?

(652) What type of mortgage allows seniors aged 62 and over the ability to withdraw equity from their homes on a monthly basis?

(653) When an investor buys securities and sells them without paying for the purchase, then he has committed what trading violation?

(654) When you buy an option, you pay the seller a nonrefundable amount, known as what?

(655) Which interest rate describes the rate you earn on an investment minus the rate of inflation?

(656) Which month is typically the worst month of the year for the Dow Jones, S&P 500, and NASDAQ?

(657) Some of the new quarters from which U.S. state contain a printing error that makes them especially valuable?

(658) The face of former U.S. President Ulysses S. Grant can be found on which U.S. bill?

(659) A certificate of deposit offered for sale by a financial advisor—rather than directly through the issuing financial institution—is referred to by what name?

(660) What are the top two most counterfeited U.S. bills of currency?

(661) What are the two primary methods (or analyses) for analyzing a stock's potential return?

(662) Where was the first U.S. mint located?

(663) Which two of the following coins have plain edges—penny, nickel, dime, quarter dollar, half dollar, presidential dollar, or Native American dollar coin?

(664) Which countries are the top two leading foreign holders of U.S. Treasury securities?

(665) Which type of retirement account provides for tax-free withdrawals under normal conditions? (a) Traditional IRA, (b) SEP IRA, (c) Roth IRA

(666) Who is the biggest holder of U.S. government debt?

(667) The abbreviation WACC is the rate at which a company is expected to pay—on average—all its security holders to finance its assets. What does WACC stand for?

(668) The total number of open (long and short) contracts in any particular commodity or options market on any given day is called what?

(669) What are the three primary accounting statements used by corporations?

(670) What does "ATM" stand for?

(671) What does the acronym ESOP stand for?

(672) A "Green-back" in another name for what?

(673) Who is responsible to a corporation for keeping track of investors that own the corporation's stocks and bonds and whether those securities are registered in the name of an individual investor or a brokerage firm?

(674) Which Federal Reserve District is the nation's largest by area and population, covering 1.3 million square miles (36% of the nation's area) and 60 million people?

(675) Which type of IRA allows persons to make contributions past age 70 1/2?

(676) Who is the top provider of workplace retirement savings plans and the largest manager of 401(k) plan assets in the United States?

(677) Who legally owns the assets in UTMA and UGMA accounts?

(678) 401k plans are associated with the private sector. What type of similar plan (i.e. tax sheltered annuity) is associated with the non-profit sector?

(679) True/False: A U.S. penny costs more than a cent to make.

(680) This program protects investors in certain securities from financial harm if a broker-dealer collapses but does not protect against losses in the securities markets, identity theft, or other 3rd-party fraud. Name this program.

(681) True/False: A stock split itself creates profits.

(682) What arrangement directs commission generated by a transaction in a client account towards a third party brokerage firm in exchange for services that are for the benefit of the client but are not client directed?

(683) What does the accounting abbreviation COGS stand for?

(684) What does the ratio GBP/USD measure?

(685) Which is higher—real returns or total returns?

(686) A "best efforts" contract and "firm commitment" contract are both associated with what general transaction?

(687) At what age are people allowed to make an extra $1,000 catch-up contribution to their IRA?

(688) At what age must people begin to take required minimum distributions, otherwise known as RMDs?

(689) Expressed as a percentage, this ratio is the rate at which a company distributes earnings to its shareholders in the form of dividends. Name this ratio.

(690) What "number" is an unofficial earnings estimate for a particular company that a stock analyst shares with clients to supplement the official published estimate?

(691) What are the two most commonly used statistical measures of risk for any share of stock?

(692) What does "DRIP" stand for?

(693) What is the formal name for employer sponsored retirement plans that meet requirements established by the Internal Revenue Service and the U.S. Congress?

(694) What does the designation "CFP" stand for?

(695) A SEP is a qualified retirement plan set up as an individual retirement account (IRA) in an employee's name. What does SEP stand for?

(696) APR is the total cost of credit over a whole year, including interest rate and fees. What does APR stand for?

(697) Corporations either report financials on a calendar year basis or what other basis?

(698) For the most part, are short-term capital gains or long-term capital gains taxed at a higher rate?

(699) In what year did the U.S. first begin minting its own coins? (a) 1776, (b) 1792, (c) 1801, (d) 1812, (e) 1865

(700) What does "TARP," a program of the United States government to purchase assets and equity from financial institutions, stand for?

(701) What does BRIC stand for?

(702) What expense are you saving for if you were to contribute to a 529 plan?

(703) What is the name for the type of capital that is considered the core measure of a bank's financial strength consisting primarily of common stock, disclosed reserves (or retained earnings), and non-redeemable non-cumulative preferred stock?

(704) What is the credit level (as defined by letters) where junk or non-investment grade status begins for bonds?

(705) As of 2013, which of the following countries holds more U.S. Treasury securities—Brazil, Germany, or Taiwan?

(706) At what price are commodities and foreign currencies sold for immediate delivery with payment in cash?

(707) Fill in the blanks: A _____ _____ is a paper document that represents ownership in a corporation.

(708) How do you calculate a bond's current yield?

(709) M0, M1, M2, and M3 are measurements of what?

(710) What does IRA stand for?

(711) What is the current trade settlement period for stocks in days?

(712) What is the Latin inscription (translated as "out of many, one") that United States law requires on every minted coin?

(713) What is the name for the calendar-related anomaly in the financial markets where stock prices—particularly those of small companies—increase in the month of January?

(714) What is the name of the thick booklet investors are given when they open an options account?

(715) If there is no activity in a client's brokerage account, how often must the brokerage firm send an account statement to its customer by law?

(716) If you own common stock in a U.S. corporation, then you have the right to vote on certain company policies and elect the board of directors by casting what?

(717) If you were to bounce a check, your bank would most likely charge you an NSF fee. What does NSF stand for?

(718) In what cities are the four facilities of the U.S. mint located?

(719) Name two of the seven states with no state tax on personal income from dividends and interest.

(720) What is the name for an order to buy a security whereby a floor broker must immediately execute the entire order at the limit price or better or else cancel the order?

(721) What is the name for the regulation that requires at least 50% equity when purchasing a share of stock?

(722) What is the name for when exchange-based commodities traders shout out their buy and sell orders or use a combination of words and hand signals to negotiate an order?

(723) In Britain, this is referred to as a cashpoint or hole in the wall. What do Americans call it?

(724) What is the typical range for FICO credit scores?

(725) When a security is offered to the public for the first time, the underwriter prepares a preliminary prospectus, otherwise known as what?

(726) In which decade during the 20th century did Fort Knox begin storing gold bullion?

(727) Normal, rather than premature, distributions from an IRA begin at what age?

(728) The day on which you buy or sell a security, option, or futures contract is called what?

(729) The penalty you owe if you withdraw money from an annuity or mutual fund within a certain time period after purchase of the investment is called what?

(730) What is the name for the official silver bullion coin of the United States?

(731) What is the penalty for a pre-mature distribution from an IRA?

(732) What type of accounts are generally managed by commodity trading advisors?

(733) What type of an account is a "Savings Incentive Match Plans for Employees"?

(734) Which bank is the largest home mortgage lender as of 2013?

# CHAPTER 7

# HISTORY AND EVENTS

## Monumental Moments in Wall Street History

*" The years teach much which days never know. "*

– RALPH WALDO EMERSON

*" Markets invariably move to undervalued and overvalued extremes because human nature falls victim to greed and/or fear. "*

– BILL GROSS

(735) Brothers Nelson Bunker Hunt and William Herbert Hunt were estimated to hold one-third (not including governmental holdings) of the entire world supply of what commodity in the late 1970s?

(736) How many regional telecommunication companies were created in the wake of the Ma Bell breakup?

(737) In 1958, Bank of America launched its own credit card named BankAmericard, but subsequently gave up control in 1970. What is this credit card called today?

(738) In 1971, this stock market opened for its first day of trading thus becoming the first electronic stock market in the world. Name this stock market.

(739) In July 2007, the SEC approved a rule change allowing companies moving from the New York Stock Exchange to the NASDAQ to retain what?

(740) Individual retirement accounts (IRAs) were introduced in what year with the enactment of the Employee Retirement Income Security Act (ERISA)? (a) 1949, (b) 1955, (c) 1964, (d) 1974, (e) 1986

(741) Name the largest bank in Canada and whose U.S. operations were purchased in June 2011 by PNC Financial Services for $3.45 billion.

(742) On August 28, 1907, two teenagers with $100 and one bicycle founded the American Messenger Company in Seattle, Washington. What is the modern name for this company?

(743) On January 31, 2011, Alpha Natural Resources acquired which troubled coal producer—itself the recipient of the largest fine for a mine accident in U.S. history—for $7.1 billion?

(744) The first index mutual fund was created in 1971 by which bank?

(745) This person was caught swindling money from others in a scheme involving the sale of international postal coupons. Who is he?

(746) True/False: Richard Whitney, former president of the New York Stock Exchange, was expelled from the exchange and later sentenced to five to ten years in Sing Sing for grand larceny.

(747) U.S. consumers purchased approximately 5 million automobiles the year of the 1929 crash. About what percentage did auto sales drop three years later in 1932 at the height of the Great Depression?

(748) What do Signature Bank of New York, Old National Bancorp of Evansville, Iberiabank of Lafayette, and Bank of Marin Bancorp of Novato all have in common?

(749) What now common technological innovation was introduced by the NYSE in 1996?

(750) Which pizza company with close to $1.7 billion in annual sales was started in 1960 by Tom Manahan in Ypsilanti, Michigan and now is headquartered in Ann Arbor, Michigan?

(751) Which carmaker division was not only the first to create vehicles that had rear turning signals with a flasher, but also to produce a car with a V6 engine?

(752) Which department store was acquired by Dayton-Hudson in 1990 and later sold to Macy's in 2004?

(753) Which major U.S. airline filed for bankruptcy protection in November, 2011?

(754) The beginnings of which Calabasas Hills, California, company began as a small cheesecake shop in Detroit, Michigan, in the late 1950s?

(755) Which U.S. corporation holds the title, without adjusting for inflation, of reporting six of the top seven largest annual earnings of all time?

(756) Approximately how many years did it take for the Dow Jones Industrial Average to surpass its 1929 peak after the crash as measured by inflation-adjusted dollars?

(757) In what city was the first Costco store opened?

(758) In 1976, this commodity futures contract defaulted thus becoming the largest default in commodities futures trading history. Name this commodity.

(759) Name the two once-dominant American photo/camera companies that each filed for Chapter 11 bankruptcy protection in the 2000s.

(760) In 1980, the *Wall Street Journal* added a second section to its newspaper. What section did it add?

(761) In what year did a bomb explode in the basement of the World Trade Center?

(762) Name the "Four Horsemen of the Stock Market Boom" of the 1920s.

(763) In the early 2000s, General Electric CEO Jack Welch attempted to buy which company for $45 billion in a deal quashed by antitrust regulators in the European Union?

(764) On June 8, 2009, The Travelers Companies and Cisco Systems were added to the Dow Jones Industrial Average. Which two companies did they replace?

(765) On September 2, 1969, this bank installed the first ATM, initially known as a Docuteller, in the U.S. at its branch in Rockville Centre, New York. Name this bank.

(766) The Glass-Owen Act of 1908 established which system?

(767) What city defaulted on its financial debt obligations in 1978? (a) Boston, (b) Cleveland, (c) Detroit, (d) Los Angeles

(768) What company did English teacher Jerry Baldwin, history teacher Zev Siegl, and writer Gordon Bowker open in 1971?

(769) What company traded under the ticker symbol "P" prior to its current user, Pandora Media?

(770) What dubious "economic organization" was established in Bagdad, Iraq in 1960?

(771) What was the informal term used to refer to 50 popular large cap stocks on the New York Stock Exchange in the 1960s and 1970s that were widely regarded as solid buy and hold growth stocks and therefore credited with propelling the bull market of the early 1970s?

(772) Which company was added to the Dow Jones Industrial Average under the name Minnesota Mining and Manufacturing in 1976?

(773) Which money-center bank acquired JP Morgan in 2000?

(774) Which of the original seven "Baby Bells" eventually changed its name in 2000 to Verizon?

(775) Which retailer did Kmart acquire in 2005 while retaining both names?

(776) Which two East Coast regional stock exchanges did the NASDAQ acquire in 2007?

(777) Dow Chemical became the first foreign industrial company to list on which major international exchange in 1973?

(778) How many banks became insolvent in 1932 at the peak of the Great Depression?

(779) In June 1965, this company became the first REIT to be listed on the New York Stock Exchange. Name this REIT.

(780) In 2009, this company pleaded guilty to the largest health care fraud in U.S. history and received the largest criminal penalty ever levied for illegal marketing. Name this company.

(781) In what decade was the first index fund launched?

(782) Mark Madoff, the eldest son of Bernard Madoff, hung himself two years after his father's arrest as his two-year old son slept nearby. What did he use to hang himself?

(783) Name the very first credit card company in the world.

(784) On July 27, 1866, Cyrus Field completed a transatlantic cable connecting telegraph operators across the Atlantic Ocean and facilitating instantaneous communication between two leading trading cities. Name these two cities.

(785) On May 6, 2010, the Dow Jones Industrial Average lost 998 points before rebounding somewhat. By what name is this "crash" known?

(786) Philip Morris International was spun-off in 2008 by which parent company?

(787) The top three discounts retailers—Walmart, Target, and Kmart—all opened their first stores in the very same year. Which year?

(788) What was the name for the PDA device Apple debuted in 1993 that flopped and was phased out by 1998 partially because of its high price ($700+) and bulkiness?

(789) What do Pets.com, the Globe.com, eToys.com, and Boo.com have in common?

(790) What do W3Catalog and Aliweb (both launched in 1993) have in common?

(791) What innovative customer service system did the National Bank of Chicago pioneer in 1946?

(792) What was the original name for the Dow Jones Transportation Average Index?

(793) Which company was valued at $691 billion at the time of its bankruptcy thus making it the biggest American company ever to go bankrupt?

(794) Which mortgage company did Bank of America acquire in 2008 perhaps making it the worst acquisition in corporate America?

(795) Which once mega-bookstore chain declared bankruptcy and permanently closed its doors in 2011?

(796) Which U.S. Supreme Court justice resigned over his association with corporate raider Louis Wolfson?

(797) Which Wall Street firm (via its PACs, individual members or employees or owners, and those individuals' immediate families) gave the most money to Barack Obama for the 2008 presidential election campaign?

(798) How much in fines and restitution was Michael Milken ordered to pay in accordance with his plea deal?

(799) Edward Callahan invested and introduced the stock ticker in 1867. What code were the stock symbols based on?

(800) In what decade during the 20<sup>th</sup>-century were women permitted to work on the trading floor of the NYSE for the first time thus ending the tradition of men only?

(801) In what month during 2009 did the stock market bottom out from the financial crisis and bounce back?

(802) In what decade of the 20th-century did the "go-go" years in the stock market occur?

(803) Name the first company to base its shareholder cash dividend on company performance, paying shareholders a once-a-year dividend calculated using a profit/growth methodology.

(804) On July 8, 1932, the Dow Jones Industrial Average reached its lowest point of the Great Depression closing at 41.22. From its peak in 1929, what percentage was the Dow Jones down on that July day in 1932?

(805) On what date did the Black Thursday crash of 1929 occur?

(806) On what exchange were stock index futures first established in 1982?

(807) True or False: In the late 1980s, a 24-inch diameter bell from 1903, presumably put away because it was too loud, was discovered in a crawl space above the main trading floor of the New York Stock Exchange.

(808) The first of this type of investment was introduced by J.P. Morgan in 1927 for the British retailer Selfridges. What kind of investment is this?

(809) This company was the first American company to issue baseball cards with a stick of gum. Name this company.

(810) What mammoth engineering project—coined the "Big Ditch"—propelled Wall Street to become the financial center of America?

(811) Which American oil and gas company did Exxon acquire in 1999?

(812) Which bank acquired BankAmerica in 1998 in what was then the largest bank acquisition in history?

(813) Which company became the first United States oil company approved by the United States Department of Interior to drill in Alaska?

(814) Which events caused brokers at the NYSE to sing either "Dixie" or "John Brown's Body" on the floor of the exchange?

(815) Which S&P 500 constituent company acquired Kinko's in February 2004?

(816) Which troubled discount brokerage firm did H&R Block acquire in 1999?

(817) Who is considered the very first capitalist to achieve a nationwide monopoly in an industry?

(818) Which video-sharing company, launched officially in November 2005, was acquired by Google for $1.65 billion one year later in November 2006?

(819) After failing to takeover CBS, Ted Turner succeeded in taking over which other media company?

(820) Approximately how many points on the Dow Jones did the market fall after the U.S. House of Representatives rejected the Bush Administration's proposed $700 billion bailout for American banks on September 29, 2008?

(821) Founded in 1865, this brokerage firm was sold to General Electric in 1986 and then sold, after suffering heavy losses, to PaineWebber in 1994. Name this firm that saw its 130-year presence on Wall Street end.

(822) In 1960, President Eisenhower signed the Cigar Tax Excise Tax Extension Act which contained a provision to stop double taxation of what type of investment?

(823) In what year did a bomb explode on Wall Street outside the NYSE building killing 33 people and injuring more than 400?

(824) In what year did crude oil hit its all-time peak price per barrel?

(825) On September 29, 1982, a scare began when the first of seven individuals died in metropolitan Chicago after ingesting which over-the-counter medicine from Johnson & Johnson?

(826) In what year did the New York Stock Exchange move into its current building at 18 Broad Street? (a) 1903, (b) 1914, (c) 1928, (d) 1947, (e) 1975

(827) On which stock exchange did the first ETF in the United States begin trading?

(828) The fall and scandal surrounding Enron lead to the dissolution of what accounting firm?

(829) The Philadelphia Stock Exchange and New York Stock Exchange were the first two stock exchanges to be established in the United States. Name the third oldest stock exchange, established in 1834.

(830) In 2008, NYSE Euronext completed a merger with what exchange for $260 million in stock and the proceeds from the sale of its headquarters?

(831) This company, founded by Marc Andreessen and Jim Clark in 1994, once commanded a 90% share of the web browser market only to see its share fall to below 1% by 2006. Name this company.

(832) What stock trading feature was banned by U.S. regulators from 1946 to 1947?

(833) What two commodity-related factors are blamed for contributing to the 1973 recession?

(834) Which company acquired Bear Stearns in 2008?

(835) Which company created the first private-sector pension plan in the United States?

(836) Which company did Time Warner acquire in 2001 for a whopping $111 billion?

(837) Which large American brokerage house was acquired by Swiss bank UBS in 2000?

(838) Which technology company was formally acquired in 2010 by Oracle Corporation for $7.4 billion?

(839) Which U.S. corporation became the first company in the world to surpass the $100 billion mark in annual sales?

(840) Who acquired National City Bank in 2008?

(841) Automated trading on the NYSE was initiated on September 25, 1995. What was the first stock traded?

(842) Cable giant Comcast stunned the world with a proposed $54 billion stock-swap bid for which company in February 2004—only to withdraw the bid three months later?

(843) In 1980, this corporation received a $1.5 billion loan from the U.S. government to keep the company afloat. Name this company.

(844) In 1994, K. Aufhauser & Company made Wall Street history by doing what?

(845) In what year did the American Stock Exchange and Toronto Stock Exchange establish the first electronic linkage between two primary equity markets in different countries?

(846) In what year did the trading in fractions end and the trading in decimals begin?

(847) In what year did the United States drop the gold standard and thus stop redeeming its paper currency for gold?

(848) Paul Thayer, deputy secretary of defense in the Reagan Administration, resigned in January 1984 due to allegations he was involved in what unlawful activity?

(849) TD Waterhouse was purchased by which discount brokerage firm in the mid-2000s?

(850) The 2010 Deepwater Horizon oil spill was commonly known by what other name?

(851) The FDA ban on saccharin in 1977 caused sharp stock drops in which two companies?

(852) The recall by Ford Motor Company of 6.5 million Firestone tires fitted to the Ford Explorer SUV culminated in the resignation of which Ford CEO?

(853) This mutual fund, now part of Vanguard, was the first balanced mutual fund in the United States and one of the oldest surviving mutual funds. Name this mutual fund established in 1928 by Walter L. Morgan with $100,000 raised from relatives and business associates.

(854) In 1936, this company became the first to affix a name-brand label to the outside of clothing. Name this company.

(855) What do Charles Dow, Edward Jones, and Charles Bergstresser have in common?

(856) What was the first modern mutual fund in the United States?

(857) Which company purchased AT&T in 2005 for more than $16 billion, but opted to keep the more iconic AT&T name?

(858) Which company was given a controlling interest in Chrysler by the U.S. government following the decision to seek bankruptcy protection?

(859) Which large money center bank reported a $2 billion trading loss in its "Chief Investment Office" in May, 2012?

(860) Which U.K. bank, established in 1762, collapsed in 1995 after one of its traders, Nick Leeson, lost $1.3 billion from speculative trading, primarily in Nikkei futures contracts, at the bank's Singapore office?

(861) Which United States "Act" of 1934 outlawed most private possession of gold, forcing individuals to sell gold to the Treasury, after which it was stored in depository at Fort Knox and other locations?

(862) Who closed on the acquisition of computer security company McAfee in 2011 for $7.68 billion?

(863) In what year did the Dow Jones Industrial Average drop 508 points, a 22.6% loss in a single day, and the second-biggest one-day drop in history?

(864) Before Genpact Limited was granted the right to trade under the ticker symbol "G", what company used the ticker symbol?

(865) During the financial crisis, to whom did Citigroup sell a majority stake in its Smith Barney brokerage unit?

(866) In 1981, this company became the first federally-funded institution to move to the private sector. Name this company.

(867) In the past, a single company could have many different ticker symbols as they varied between the dozens of individual stock markets. Which company was responsible for developing the modern letter-only ticker symbols whereby each stock was identified by only one ticker?

(868) In what year was AT&T's local operations split into seven independent Regional Holding Companies, also known as Regional Bell Operating Companies (RBOCs), or "Baby Bells"?

(869) In what year was the most expensive inflation-adjusted seat sold on the New York Stock Exchange?

(870) Prior to using the now famous bell, what device was used to signal the opening of trading on the New York Stock Exchange?

(871) The Arab oil embargo occurred in which year?

(872) The Banking Act of 1933 (Glass-Steagall) created what corporation to safeguard deposits held at banks?

(873) The first attempt at a national currency occurred in 1775 when the Continental Congress began issuing its own paper currency. What was the name given to this currency?

(874) The trading of what type of securities were banned on May 11, 1861?

(875) True/False: The first telephones were installed on the floor of the trading floor in 1929.

(876) Which 19th-century Wall Street scandal implicated U.S. President Grant's vice president and certain key cabinet members?

(877) Which American colony became the first in the United States to issue paper currency in 1690?

(878) Which company nearly purchased the Chrysler Group from Cerberus Capital in 2008 before ending talks due to a worsening cash position?

(879) Which company renamed itself to Scottrade in 2000 due to the success of its online brokerage operations?

(880) Which county declared Chapter 9 bankruptcy on December 6, 1994, as a result of losses from leveraged bond strategies employed by Robert Citron?

(881) Which stock exchange did the NASDAQ attempt—but ultimately fail—to acquire between 2005-2007?

(882) Who became the first company to issue its earnings reports in comic book form?

(883) Who acquired Chrysler in 1999 for $37 billion and resold the company for a mere $7 billion a few years later to Cerberus Capital?

(884) Who did the NASDAQ purchase for $652 million on November 7th, 2007?

(885) As of 2013, which brokerage firm has more registered representatives (financial advisors) than any other firm?

(886) Du Pont was ordered to divest itself of what stock in 1957?

(887) How many points did the Dow Jones Industrial Average fall during the 1929 crash on October 4th?

(888) In 1996, what significant event occurred in regards to stock quotes used on television?

(889) In what year did the NYSE close for four months and two weeks—the longest exchange shutdown on record?

(890) In what year did the NYSE register as a national securities exchange with the United States Securities and Exchange Commission?

(891) In what year where distinguished guests first permitted to ring the opening bell to signal the start of trading on the NYSE?

(892) The "Big Five" was the name given to a group of companies that wielded considerable political power in the Territory of Hawaii during the early 20th-century. In what type of business were these companies involved?

(893) In which city did Ray Kroc open his first McDonald's restaurant?

(894) The firm Scudder, Stevens and Clark is best known as the first to launch what type of investment in 1928?

(895) The Glass–Steagall Act regulated the separation of what two industries/functions?

(896) The trading of what major investment product did the American Stock Exchange launch in 1975?

(897) This U.S. cable news channel, founded in 1980 by Ted Turner, was the first channel to provide 24-hour television news coverage and the first all-news television channel in the United States. Name this channel.

(898) Victoria Woodhull and Tennessee Claflin are considered the first to accomplish what feat?

(899) Which American brewing company, now part of the Pabst Brewing Company, was once the largest producer of beer in the world with its namesake beer known as "The beer that made Milwaukee famous"?

(900) Which American company holds the record as the largest initial public offering in the United States?

(901) Which company was the first to offer shares of its common stock as part of its pension fund?

(902) Which investment firm acquired Dean Witter Reynolds in the 1990s?

(903) Which major investment firm did Bank of America acquire in 2008?

(904) Which S&P 500 constituent company typically kicks off earnings season for major companies?

(905) Who introduced the UNIVAC I (UNIVersal Automatic Computer I), the first commercial computer made in the United States?

(906) Without adjusting for inflation, which U.S. corporation holds the unfortunate title of reporting the largest annual corporate loss of all time at nearly $100 billion in 2008?

(907) "Black Tuesday" is the name given to the single biggest one-day fall in the Dow Jones Industrial Average during the crash of 1929. On what date did "Black Tuesday" occur?

(908) Aviation stocks experienced a significant rally in 1927. What historical event was the catalyst for this rally?

(909) How many trading sessions were closed as a result of the September 11, 2001, terrorist attacks on the World Trade Center?

(910) In 2001, this carmaker became the first in North America to sell a new type of automobile known as a hybrid. Name this company.

(911) In 1914, the NYSE closed for the first time since 1873. What event caused this closure?

(912) In what year was the NYSE closed every Wednesday during the second half of the year to deal with a "Paperwork Crisis"?

(913) In which company did Warren Buffett's Berkshire Hathaway invest $5 billion in August 2011 thus giving banks a jolt of investor confidence?

(914) John Maynard Keynes compared the Great Depression to what other era in the history of Western civilization?

(915) Name the first American company to make golf balls.

(916) The Federal Reserve was not the first "national bank" of the United States. How many preceded—yet failed— before the current Federal Reserve took hold?

(917) The Securities Act of 1933 is associated with which securities market? (a) Primary, (b) Secondary, (c) Third, (d) Fourth

(918) The stock market plunged in 1881 after the shooting of what U.S. president?

(919) This company, the seventh largest corporation in the United States circa 1900, is the only company of the original twelve in the Dow Jones Industrial Average to dissolve. Name this company.

(920) What historic event occurred on April 30, 1789, on the balcony of Federal Hall located on Wall Street?

(921) What company changed its name to Venator Group in 1997 and to Foot Locker in 2001?

(922) Which bank acquired Chase Manhattan bank in 1996 but took on the more prominent Chase name?

(923) Which company sold more than 800 patents to Microsoft for $1.056B in April of 2012?

(924) Which company, an original twelve of the Dow Jones Industrial Average, changed its name to Uniroyal in 1961, merged with private B.F. Goodrich in 1986, and was bought by Michelin in 1990?

(925) Which Japanese carmaker did Ford rescue in 1996 by pumping in nearly $500 million thus marking the first American company to take control of a Japanese carmaker?

(926) Which multi-billion dollar corporation—formed by the merger of two once-great railroads, went bankrupt in 1970?

(927) Who did Facebook attempt—but ultimately fail—to acquire for $500 million in cash and stock in late 2008?

(928) Who is the only American president to completely pay off the national debt?

(929) As of the end of 2012, what is the all-time peak on the Dow Jones Industrial Average?

(930) In 1968, this company became the first coffee company in the United States to begin packaging coffee in vacuum-packed foil bags. Name this company.

(931) Financial journalist Alfred W. Jones is credited with the creation of what in 1949?

(932) In 1932, U.S. GNP was approximately $42 billion. How did this figure compare to the GNP of 1929, the year of the crash?

(933) In 2001, VoiceStream Wireless PCS was acquired by Deutsche Telekom and renamed to what in July 2002?

(934) Which company had a larger IPO—Facebook or General Motors?

(935) Name the first American company to stand trial in a U.S. court for alleged human rights violations committed abroad.

(936) Name the first true global bank.

(937) Of the companies included in the Dow Jones Industrial Average, which one has the longest tenure in the index?

(938) The first African American to head a Fortune 500 company was Franklin Raines. Which company did he run?

(939) This person is a former CEO of Tyco International, convicted in 2005 of crimes related to his receipt of $81 million in purportedly unauthorized bonuses and the purchase of art for $14.7 million. Name him.

(940) This multi-strategy hedge fund founded by Nicholas Maounis and headquartered in Greenwich, Connecticut, collapsed in September 2006 after losing in excess of $5 billion on natural gas futures making it one of the largest known trading losses and hedge fund collapses in history. Name this hedge fund.

(941) What company spun-off Yum! Brands in 1997?

(942) This person was the first Treasury secretary and architect of the early United States financial system. Name this person buried in the cemetery of Trinity Church.

(943) What is the name given to the bubble and eventual pop of the early 2000s principally related to the NASDAQ?

(944) Which bankruptcy reorganization did General Motors go through in the late 2000s?

(945) Which company was added to the Dow Jones Industrial Average under the name Aluminum Company of America in 1959?

(946) Which hedge fund associated with Myron Scholes and Robert C. Merton, who shared the 1997 Nobel Memorial Prize in Economic Sciences, closed in 2000 after losing $4.6 billion in less than four months following the Russian financial crisis and requiring financial intervention by the Federal Reserve?

(947) Which major credit rating agency downgraded its rating on U.S. sovereign debt in 2011?

(948) Which of the following three investment products were created first? (a) Exchange-Traded Funds, (b) Hedge Funds, (c) Mutual Funds

(949) Who spun-off Avaya in October 2000?

(950) Who was the first Wall Street company to pay back loaned TARP bailout money?

# CHAPTER 8

# MISCELLANEA AND ODDITIES
## Little Known Facts and the Strange but True

*" When written in Chinese the word crisis is composed of two characters. One represents danger and the other represents opportunity. "*

– JOHN F. KENNEDY

*" In theory there is no difference between theory and practice. In practice there is. "*

– YOGI BERRA

(951) Who directed the 1987 film *Wall Street*?

(952) *Every Man His Own Broker*, a book published in 1775, contained the first usage of what two words now synonymous with making and losing money on Wall Street?

(953) Wall Street got its name from a 1340-foot wood wall erected by Governor Peter Stuyvesant to keep pigs and goats out. In what century was this wall erected?

(954) What was the original name for the television channel CNBC until 1991?

(955) Which state boasts more corporate headquarters (at least on paper) than any other state in America?

(956) William Shatner plays the role of "Negotiator" in which company's advertisements?

(957) At the end of the movie *Wall Street*, when Bud Fox gets out of the car to take the long walk up the stairs to the court room, he passes by a newspaper stand in the background with a poster for *Fortune* magazine. Who is on the cover of Fortune?

(958) Director Oliver Stone's first two choices to play Gordon Gekko in the movie *Wall Street* were Richard Gere and Warren Beatty. Who did he ultimately select?

(959) Fill in the blank: "Buy on rumors, sell on _____."

(960) In which movie is James Carney forced to sell his taxicabs to satisfy a margin call?

(961) In which Wall Street related movie did Eddie Murphy star as both a bum and trader?

(962) Fill in the blank: "Bulls make money. Bears make money. _____ get slaughtered."

(963) True/False: Companies are no longer required to issue paper stock certificates.

(964) Finish this line from character Gordon Gekko in the film *Wall Street*, "Greed is _____."

(965) Into which hall of fame were the four founders of Harley-Davidson inducted?

(966) The Conference Board is one of two organizations that track and measure consumer confidence. Name the second organization.

(967) Founded in 1888, this international business newspaper is published in London and printed in 24 cities around the world. Name this highly respected newspaper.

(968) Founded in 1984 by William O'Neil and headquartered in Los Angeles, this national newspaper published Monday through Friday goes by the acronym IBD. Name this newspaper.

(969) *Barbarians at the Gate* is a book based on the accounts surrounding the leveraged buyout of which firm?

(970) The origin of this corporate name was derived from the words "Equitable" and "Factual." Name this company.

(971) True or False: *Wall Street* was the first feature film to demonstrate the use of a cordless phone.

(972) In 2012, CNBC became the first media entity to have a permanent broadcast stage on the trading floor of the NYSE. What "post number" does it occupy?

(973) In the movie *Wall Street*, what birthday gift did Bud Fox bring on his first meeting with Gordon Gekko?

(974) The CFA designation is arguably the top professional credential any money manager or investment advisor can earn. What does CFA stand for?

(975) This newspaper was established in 1889 under the name Customer's Afternoon Letter. What is the modern name?

(976) What does "S.O.S.", as in S.O.S. scrub pads stand for?

(977) In the movie *Wall Street*, after whom did Michael Douglas model his performance as Gordon Gekko?

(978) McDonald's stopped offering spoon-shaped coffee stirrers because they were being inappropriately used as what?

(979) The completion of which exam (in addition to the Series 63) allows a financial advisor to sell mutual funds, but not stocks?

(980) Fill in the blank: "The _____ is your friend."

(981) What does the cable channel ESPN stand for?

(982) Is a 50-day moving average trend line or 200-day moving average trend line typically more volatile?

(983) Name the commodity (e.g. coffee) the characters played by Eddie Murphy and Dan Aykroyd in the movie *Trading Places* are attempting to corner near the end of the movie.

(984) The *Wall Street Journal* has a daily column called; "_____ on the Street"

(985) What is the name for Jim Cramer's CNBC evening program?

(986) What is the name of the program on CNBC that highlights true stories of conmen and Ponzi schemes?

(987) Name the top two largest University endowments in the United States as of 2013.

(988) On which day of the week is the Initial (jobless) Claims report released?

(989) What are the two most important economic indicators released in the monthly jobs report?

(990) What is the name for someone or something that is used to describe a friendly party that buys the shares of one organization to help prevent against a hostile takeover of that organization by another party?

(991) Which actor apparently wanted to play the part of Bud Fox—a role already given to Charlie Sheen by Oliver Stone—in the movie *Wall Street*?

(992) The English word "cash" originated from a Latin word meaning "money box". Name this Latin word.

(993) The face of former U.S. President William McKinley can be found on which U.S. bill?

(994) What is the name for the body of elected or appointed members who jointly oversee the activities of a company or organization?

(995) Which popular financial magazine was founded by *TIME* co-founder Henry Luce in February 1930, four months after the Wall Street Crash of 1929?

(996) According to Phoenix Marketing International, which U.S. state had the highest percentage of millionaire households of total state households for the year 2011?

(997) This novel, written by Bret Easton Ellis, follows the day-to-day life of a Wall Street investment banker and serial killer. What is the name of the novel?

(998) What is the statistical measure of when the market prices for two stocks move relatively the same?

(999) Which actor in the movie *Wall Street* has never seen the film she co-starred in?

(1000) Who owns *Barron's* and has published it since 1921?

(1001) Who starred as a Wall Street tycoon in the movie *Sabrina*?

# CHAPTER 9

# ANSWERS TO ALL QUESTIONS

1. Charging Bull (by Arturo Di Modica)

2. *Random*

3. Mining and oil

4. (a) 1966

5. Meredith Whitney

6. Cornelius Vanderbilt

7. Joseph Seligman

8. Irving Fisher

9. The Bancroft family

10. Warren E. Buffett

11. H. Ross Perot

12. Muriel Siebert

13. Pennsylvania

14. Ronald Reagan

15. 150

16. Lombard Street

17. Barton Biggs

18. John C. Bogle

19. Steve Ballmer

20. The Trump Building

21. Arthur Laffer ("Laffer Curve")

22. Bernard Baruch

23. Paul A. Volcker

24. Madison Square Garden

25. McKesson Corporation

26. Rupert Murdoch

27. Credit rating agencies

28. Ben Bernanke

29. Dr. Kenneth "Ken" Lay

30. Daniels & Bell, Inc.

31. Chevrolet

32. Illiteracy

33. Andrew Carnegie and Andrew Mellon

34. Bill Gross

35. Ronald Reagan (in 1985)

36. Dominique Strauss-Kahn

37. College dropouts

38. One-car garage

39. Steamboats and railroads

40. *Gloom Boom & Doom Report*

41. Angela Merkel

42. John Thain

43. Bob Seger

44. Got married

45. J. P. Morgan

46. Paul Allen and Bill Gates

47. Louis Rukeyser

48. Joseph P. Kennedy

49. Ohio

50. Fur trading

51. Virgin Atlantic Airways Ltd.

52. Henry Ford (offered to sell Ford Motor Company)

53. California, Texas, and New York

54. Blasting powder

55. First president of the New York Stock Exchange

56. Salomon Brothers

57. Bain Capital

58. Lawrence J. "Larry" Ellison

59. Tom Monoghan

60. Ivan Boesky

61. Jack Grubman

62. Massachusetts

63. New York Stock Exchange

64. Florida

65. Prince Al-Waleed bin Talal

66. San Francisco

67. 40 Wall Street (The Trump Building)

68. Bill & Melinda Gates

69. Exelon

70. Walter F. Tellier

71. Joseph L. Searles III

72. Michael R. Milken

73. JPMorgan Chase

74. Ford Motor Company

75. Houston

76. Broadway and South Street

77. Mark Cuban

78. Andrew Carnegie

79. Fidelity Magellan

80. TheStreet.com

81. Jon Corzine

82. Henry Ford, John Rockefeller, and Andrew Mellon

83. CNBC

84. Tennessee

85. Financials/Banks

86. Ben & Jerry's

87. Delaware

88. Gretchen Schoenleber

89. Sam Walton

90. Richard Grasso

91. Carly Fiorina

92. Andrew W. Mellon and John D. Rockefeller

93. Bill Gates

94. Illinois

95. 11 Wall Street

96. Maryland

97. 1929 stock market crash

98. James (Jim) Rogers

99. North Carolina

100. Founders of Apple Computer

101. Adam Smith

102. Deutsche Bank (at 60 Wall Street)

103. Mark Haines

104. Lawrence "Larry" Kudlow

105. Allstate Insurance

106. New Hampshire

107. Steelmaking

108. Harvard University

109. Harlow Curtice

110. Maria Bartiromo

111. Ted Turner

112. NeXT Computer

113. Cornelius Vanderbilt

114. Drexel Burnham Lambert

115. Jeff Bezos

116. Board

117. Standard & Poor's

118. 2005 (December 6)

119. 9:40am

120. Edward Jones, a statistician

121. First use of tickers (symbols) and ticker tapes

122. Chicago Stock Exchange

123. Exchange-listed stocks

124. Pacific Commodities Exchange

125. 4:00pm ET

126. (d) 52%

127. (d) 1906 (on January 12)

128. 1957

129. Wednesday

130. United Kingdom

131. NYSE Composite Index

132. Philadelphia Stock Exchange

133. Fourth Market

134. 9:30am ET

135. False

136. 1792

137. Germany

138. 12

139. Gross Domestic Product (GDP)

140. James J. Needham

141. Toronto Stock Exchange (TSX, formerly TSE)

142. Lowest volume date recorded with only 31 shares traded.

143. Small-cap stocks

144. Mid caps

145. Cross listed

146. Circuit breaker rule

147. Missouri (Kansas City Fed and St. Louis Fed)

148. 1984

149. 1954

150. True. XL Group plc

151. The Curb

152. (b) 1848

153. Wilshire 5000 Total Market Index

154. (a) Chicago Board of Trade

155. National Association of Securities Dealers Automated Quotation

156. South Africa

157. Midwest Stock Exchange

158. Selling short

159. Federal Reserve Bank of Richmond and San Francisco

160. Leading Indicators

161. Canada

162. Consolidated Stock and Petroleum Exchange of New York

163. American Stock Exchange

164. The Census Bureau of the Department of Commerce

165. About $15.5 trillion

166. The Employment and Training Administration of the Department of Labor

167. 2,300

168. 30%

169. World War I

170. Began wearing brightly colored jackets and hats

171. Belgium

172. Odd lot

173. Index of Leading Economic Indicators

174. 1975

175. There are no requirements

176. Chicago Board of Trade

177. Limit order

178. Four (located in each of the four main sections/rooms of the NYSE)

179. 30

180. New York Stock & Exchange Board

181. Dow Jones Transportation Average (DJIA)

182. Sarbanes–Oxley, or simply Sarbox or SOX

183. 1366

184. False

185. New York Stock Exchange

186. Tender offer

187. Stop loss order

188. Detroit

189. Three

190. Odd lots

191. North American Free Trade Agreement (NAFTA)

192. Good 'til canceled

193. Single-family home prices

194. Commodity Futures Trading Commission

195. London Stock Exchange

196. Over 100% higher

197. Bay Street (Toronto)

198. Montreal Stock Exchange and Canadian Stock Exchange

199. Rage Against the Machine

200. (e) 1972 (on November 14)

201. Delisted

202. Consumer Price Index

203. Railroads

204. Canadian Maple Leaf

205. Affordable Care Act

206. About 4,100

207. Five

208. 1999 (on March 29)

209. 2008 (October 10, 2008)

210. Australian Securities Exchange (ASX)

211. Dow Jones Industrial Average

212. NASDAQ-100

213. Nikkei Stock Average

214. Chicago Board of Trade

215. 200 years

216. Berkshire Hathaway Class A

217. Phillips Petroleum

218. Berkshire Hathaway, Inc.

219. Government National Mortgage Association

220. Urban Outfitters, Inc.

221. Transamerica

222. General Motors (in 1955)

223. National Futures Association (NFA)

224. Sears

225. Merck & Co., Inc.

226. International Business Machines Corporation (IBM)

227. Transocean

228. Time Warner (formerly AOL Time Warner)

229. Costco

230. Bank of New York

231. World Bank

232. Royal Dutch Shell plc

233. SLM Corporation

234. The Federal Reserve System (also known as the Federal Reserve, and informally as the Fed)

235. Washington, D.C.

236. Ford

237. Marathon Oil Corporation

238. Mickey Mouse

239. Sysco Corporation

240. Walmart

241. Starbucks

242. Schlumberger Limited

243. Blimp

244. Enterprise Holdings

245. Standard Oil (of Cleveland)

246. Macromedia

247. Jack in the box

248. Computershare

249. Xerox Corporation

250. Chrysler Corporation

251. Ask.com

252. Navy Federal Credit Union

253. PayPal

254. AutoNation

255. International Monetary Fund

256. Book entry

257. Certificate

258. LUV

259. Darden Restaurants

260. CME Group

261. All three—trick question!

262. Chrysler Corporation

263. Western Union

264. Royal Caribbean Cruises Ltd.

265. In-N-Out Burger

266. Allstate

267. Nabisco

268. Northwest Airlines

269. International Paper Company

270. Apollo Group, Inc.

271. U.S. Steel

272. Morgan Stanley

273. Cedar Fair LP (owner of Cedar Point)

274. Altria Group, Inc.

275. Masco Corporation

276. Comerica

277. Deutsche Bank

278. Brinker International, Inc.

279. Options Clearing Corporation (OCC)

280. General Motors

281. Government-sponsored enterprise, or GSE

282. X

283. New York Cable Railway (2 feet by 3 feet)

284. IBM

285. Sprint Nextel Corp.

286. Medtronic, Inc.

287. A.G. Edwards

288. Hospital Corporation of America (HCA)

289. J. P. Morgan

290. The Coca-Cola Company

291. International Monetary Fund

292. Stericycle

293. Nine

294. PricewaterhouseCoopers

295. Blue, as in Blue Sheets

296. Foot Locker, Inc.

297. Washington Mutual

298. Apple Computer, Inc.

299. Starwood Hotels & Resorts Worldwide

300. Diageo plc.

301. Xerox

302. Simon Property Group, Inc.

303. Pulte Homes, Inc.

304. True

305. International Paper

306. Bank of New York (Now BNY Mellon)

307. Deere & Company

308. Northrop Grumman Corporation

309. Yahoo!

310. Beige Book

311. Walgreen Co.

312. *Wall Street Journal*

313. Exxon

314. National Association of Securities Dealers, Inc. (NASD)

315. Kellogg Company

316. Benjamin Franklin

317. Three billionaires and 12,000 millionaires

318. XeroX

319. AT&T

320. Hitachi Ltd.

321. The Motley Fool

322. Boston Beer Co. Inc.

323. Fidelity Investments (or FMR LLC)

324. Whole Foods Market

325. International Game Technology

326. Symantec Corporation

327. Pension Benefit Guaranty Corporation (PBGC)

328. Moody's, Standard & Poor's, and Fitch

329. Bid price

330. Raymond James

331. Dean Witter

332. IBM

333. Fortune Brands

334. Viacom Inc.

335. Big Lots

336. Wendy's

337. State Farm Insurance

338. NCUA (National Credit Union Administration)

339. Bonds

340. Robert Half International

341. Amazon.com

342. Fourteen

343. Meta Financial Group, Inc.

344. Ford Motor Company (Henry Ford bought him out)

345. Johnson Controls

346. Toys R Us

347. Raytheon Company

348. Stanley Black & Decker

349. Bank of America

350. The Gap, Inc.

351. VF Corporation

352. Federal Reserve

353. NDAQ

354. Kohlberg, Kravis, Roberts

355. Union Pacific Railroad

356. Kmart

357. Nike

358. Dell

359. General Electric

360. Waste Management and Republic Services

361. Intel

362. United Airlines

363. First Boston

364. Bowne & Company, Inc.

365. Intuit, Inc.

366. Twelve

367. Green Bay Packers

368. 1950s

369. Fastenal Co.

370. Edward Jones

371. Ibbotson Associates

372. Freeze-dried ice cream

373. Pier 1 Imports

374. The J. M. Smucker Company

375. USX Corporation

376. Open Market Committee

377. Largest privately owned companies in the U.S.

378. Occupy Wall Street

379. FIZZ

380. Yahoo!

381. Agilent Technologies Inc.

382. Reuters

383. (b) Barnes Group

384. Twitter, Inc.

385. IBM

386. Delta Air Lines

387. MCI Worldcom

388. Hasbro

389. Exxon Mobil Corporation

390. Federal Home Loan Mortgage Corporation

391. Conoco

392. Facebook

393. Morningstar

394. Master Charge

395. The Kroger Co.

396. Comcast

397. Gannett Company

398. eBay

399. Boeing

400. Consumer Value Stores

401. Quantitative Easing

402. Smoked, dried jalapeño chili pepper

403. New York Mercantile Exchange

404. American Express preferred

405. Peabody Energy Corp.

406. Duke Energy

407. Smith Barney

408. BlackRock

409. AT&T

410. Boeing and Lockheed Martin

411. McKesson Corporation

412. Waste Management, Inc.

413. The McGraw-Hill Companies, Inc.

414. Target Corporation

415. Amgen

416. $2 per share

417. Con Edison

418. $80 million in U.S. government bonds issued in 1790 to refinance Revolutionary War debt

419. WorldCom (Now MCI and a subsidiary of Verizon Communications)

420. The Federal Reserve Bank

421. Yum! Brands, Inc.

422. Newport News Shipbuilding

423. Eli Lilly and Company

424. Caterpillar Inc.

425. Securities and Exchange Commission (SEC)

426. American Telephone & Telegraph

427. American businesses that have moved their legal addresses abroad

428. The European Common Market

429. The Organization of the Petroleum Exporting Countries

430. Kaufman and Broad Home Corporation

431. Government National Mortgage Association (Ginnie Mae)

432. IBM

433. Halliburton

434. Equifax, Experian, and TransUnion

435. Perrigo Company

436. Subway

437. Rio Tinto Group

438. Florida Power & Light

439. Mattel, Inc.

440. The Home Depot

441. 1913

442. Carnival Corporation & plc

443. NextEra Energy Resources

444. Baby Einstein

445. Plum Creek Timber

446. HWP

447. FedEx

448. CBRE Group, Inc (name change from CB Richard Ellis Group in 2011)

449. HoTMaiL

450. United Parcel Service, Inc.

451. Committee on Uniform Security Identification Procedures

452. AT&T

453. Blue Sky Laws

454. Employee Retirement Income Security Act (of 1974)

455. Charles Schwab

456. Merrill Lynch

457. The Federal Reserve Bank

458. California Public Employees' Retirement System (CalPERS)

459. Dubai

460. Positively

461. Deere (as in John Deere)

462. Maxwell House coffee

463. McDonald's

464. Campbell Soup Company

465. Verizon

466. New Coke

467. Arrow

468. Bob Evans Farms, Inc.

469. Aflac Incorporated

470. Allstate

471. Motorola

472. Neighbor

473. The J.M. Smucker Co.

474. Wheaties

475. Blue

476. Staples Inc.

477. Xerox Corporation

478. Bagels

479. 15% or more

480. Swoosh

481. America Online

482. E.F. Hutton

483. Sunoco Inc.

484. Dreyfus

485. Reese's Pieces

486. Fossil, Inc.

487. Siri

488. American Express

489. MasterCard

490. Liquid Paper

491. Jack Daniels Whiskey

492. Red bullseye

493. Burger King

494. As a wallpaper cleaner

495. Kimberly-Clark Corporation

496. Wrigley's Gum

497. Nike

498. Red umbrella

499. The North Face, Inc.

500. Harley-Davidson Motor Cycles

501. 3Com

502. General Electric

503. Prudential Financial, Inc.

504. Original Pentium processors

505. Dr. Pepper

506. Lowe's

507. Kix cereal

508. Charles E. Merrill and Edmund C. Lynch

509. Wallet

510. Groupon

511. H. J. Heinz Company

512. John Deere

513. Verizon

514. CNBC

515. SPDR S&P 500 (Symbol: SPY)

516. Bondholders

517. Morgan Stanley Capital International

518. Coupon

519. 13 and 26 week T-bills

520. Original-Issue Discount or (OID)

521. Worthless bonds

522. Jumbo CDs

523. Revenue bonds

524. Derivatives

525. Flower bonds

526. Treasury Note

527. Dow Jones Industrial Average

528. They will rise

529. NASDAQ-100

530. Consumer Price Index (CPI)

531. American Depository Receipt

532. Underwater

533. Banker's acceptance

534. Call date

535. Closed-end funds

536. Spin-off

537. Value companies

538. Options

539. Municipal bond

540. Reverse stock split

541. Interest

542. Float

543. One year

544. Naked

545. Secured bond

546. Debenture

547. Option chain or string

548. Leveraged and inverse ETFs

549. Exchange-Traded Fund

550. Class A

551. (a) open-end funds

552. Dollar-Cost Averaging

553. U.S. Treasury zero-coupon bonds

554. Efficient Market Hypothesis

555. London Interbank Offered Rate

556. Euro currency

557. Foreign currency exchange

558. Treasury stock

559. Penny stocks

560. Short squeeze

561. Brent Crude

562. Socially-responsible investing (SRI)

563. Cumulative preferred

564. Types of crude oil

565. Current ratio

566. Street name

567. Earnings Per Share

568. ETF

569. Municipal Securities Rulemaking Board

570. U.S. Treasury bills that mature in 13 weeks

571. Discount rate

572. Rollover or 401k rollover

573. Short interest

574. Dogs of the Dow

575. Nonconvertible preferred stock

576. Margin call

577. Commodity futures contracts

578. Dividend

579. Maturity date

580. Common stock

581. Real Estate Investment Trust

582. Earnings Before Interest, Taxes, Depreciation and Amortization

583. 270

584. Deflation

585. Goodwill

586. Common stock

587. Random Walk Theory

588. Margin rate

589. $1,000

590. Turnover

591. Sugar #11 is world grown and sugar #16 is U.S. grown

592. Nominal interest rate

593. Options

594. Federal Open Market Committee

595. Discount bond

596. Sell short or selling short

597. Uptick

598. Catholic values

599. Japanese Yen

600. Heating oil

601. Bonds (10-30 years)

602. Options

603. Contrarians

604. Yankee bonds

605. Insurance companies

606. Yield to Maturity

607. Municipal bonds

608. Disinflation

609. Bearer bonds

610. Put option

611. Class C

612. Strike price

613. Collateralized Mortgage Obligation

614. Over the counter

615. CUSIP

616. General obligation bonds (also called GOs)

617. An ETF (gold)

618. Street Name

619. Federal Deposit Insurance Corporation

620. Put or putable

621. Prospectus

622. Churning

623. Series 7

624. Block or block of shares

625. Commercial paper

626. Qualified

627. Treasury Inflation-Protected Securities (TIPS)

628. Divide the market price per share of common stock by the earnings per share of a corporation

629. Options

630. Eurodollars

631. Volatility

632. Warrant

633. Junk bonds

634. U.S. Treasury

635. Call option

636. SPDR Barclays Capital High Yield Bond ETF

637. All use the U.S. dollar as their legal tender exclusively

638. Quadruple witching day

639. $250,000

640. Wash sale

641. Bloomberg Terminals

642. Laddering

643. Vesting

644. Oversubscribed

645. Inverted or negative

646. M3

647. Upgrades and downgrades

648. Financial Accounting Standards Board

649. Nonsystematic risk

650. True

651. $50

652. Reverse mortgage

653. Freeriding

654. Premium or option premium

655. Real interest rate

656. September

657. Wisconsin

658. $50 bill

659. Brokered CD

660. $20, then $100

661. Fundamental and technical

662. Philadelphia

663. Penny and nickel

664. China and Japan

665. (c) Roth IRA

666. U.S. Federal Reserve and intragovernmental holdings ($6+ trillion)

667. Weighted Average Cost of Capital

668. Open interest

669. Balance sheet statement, income statement, and cash flow statement

670. Automated Teller Machine

671. Employee Stock Option Plan

672. U.S. dollar

673. Transfer agent

674. Federal Reserve Bank of San Francisco

675. Roth IRAs

676. Fidelity Investments

677. Minors (children)

678. 403b plans

679. True

680. Securities Investor Protection Corporation (SIPC)

681. False

682. Soft dollar

683. Cost of Goods Sold

684. U.S. dollars per Great Britain pound

685. Total returns

686. Initial Public Offering (IPO)

687. Age 50

688. 70 1/2

689. Payout ratio

690. Whisper number

691. Standard deviation and beta

692. Dividend Reinvestment Plan (or Program)

693. Qualified retirement plans

694. Certified Financial Planner

695. Simplified employee pension (SEP)

696. Annual Percentage Rate

697. Fiscal year

698. Short-term capital gains

699. (b) 1792

700. Troubled Asset Relief Program

701. Brazil, Russia, India, and China

702. Education

703. Tier 1 capital

704. BB or Ba

705. Brazil, and by a wide margin

706. Spot price

707. Stock certificate

708. Annual interest payments divided by current market value

709. U.S. money supply

710. Individual Retirement Account

711. T+3 (Trade date plus three days)

712. E PLURIBUS UNUM

713. January Effect

714. Characteristics and Risks of Standardized Options

715. Quarterly

716. Proxy

717. Non-Sufficient Funds

718. Philadelphia, Denver, San Francisco, and West Point

719. Alaska, Florida, Nevada, South Dakota, Texas, Washington, and Wyoming

720. Fill or kill order

721. Regulation T

722. Open outcry

723. Automated Teller Machine or ATM

724. 300 to 850 points

725. Red herring

726. 1930s (1938 to be precise)

727. 59 1/2

728. Trade date

729. Surrender fee (or charge)

730. American Silver Eagle

731. 10% of the distribution

732. Managed futures funds

733. IRA as in SIMPLE IRA

734. Wells Fargo

735. Silver

736. Seven

737. Visa

738. NASDAQ

739. Their three letter symbols

740. (d) 1974

741. Royal Bank of Canada (RBC)

742. United Parcel Service (UPS)

743. Massey Energy

744. Wells Fargo

745. Carlo Ponzi

746. True

747. Nearly 80% to 1 million in automobile sales

748. First banks to repay TARP loans

749. Real-time ticker

750. Domino's Pizza, Inc.

751. Buick (a GM division)

752. Marshall Field & Company

753. AMR (Parent of American Airlines)

754. The Cheesecake Factory, Inc.

755. ExxonMobil

756. 25 (surpassed in 1954)

757. Seattle

758. Potatoes

759. Polaroid and Eastman Kodak

760. Marketplace

761. 1993

762. General Motors, Yellow Cab, Fisher Body, and du Pont

763. Honeywell

764. General Motors and Citigroup

765. Chemical Bank

766. Federal Reserve System

767. (b) Cleveland

768. Starbucks

769. Phillips Petroleum

770. OPEC

771. Nifty Fifty

772. 3M

773. Chase Bank

774. Bell Atlantic

775. Sears

776. Boston Stock Exchange and Philadelphia Stock Exchange

777. Tokyo Stock Exchange

778. About 1,600

779. Continental Mortgage Investors

780. Pfizer, Inc.

781. 1970s

782. Dog leash

783. Diners Club

784. New York and London

785. Flash crash

786. Altria Group

787. 1962

788. Newton

789. Internet companies that failed during the dotcom bubble

790. First ever internet search engines and portals

791. Drive-in banking

792. Dow Jones Rail Average

793. Lehman Brothers in 2008

794. Countrywide Loans

795. Borders Bookstore

796. Abe Fortas

797. Goldman Sachs

798. $200 million in fines and $400 million in restitution

799. Morse code

800. 1940s (1943)

801. March

802. 1960s

803. Progressive Casualty Insurance Company

804. 89%

805. October 24th

806. Kansas City Board of Trade

807. True

808. American Depository Receipt (ADR)

809. Goudey

810. The Erie Canal

811. Mobil

812. NationsBank of Charlotte

813. Conoco Phillips

814. Announcements of either Union or Confederate victories during the Civil War

815. FedEx

816. Olde Discount Stockbrokers

817. John D. Rockefeller

818. YouTube

819. MGM/UA

820. Nearly 778 points

821. Kidder, Peabody & Co.

822. Real estate investment trusts

823. 1920 (the perpetrators were never found)

824. 2008 ($149 in July)

825. Extra Strength Tylenol

826. (a) 1903

827. American Stock Exchange

828. Arthur Andersen

829. Boston Stock Exchange

830. American Stock Exchange

831. Netscape Communications (now a subsidiary of AOL)

832. Stocks could not be purchased on margin

833. Arab oil embargo and high grain prices

834. J.P. Morgan Chase

835. American Express (in 1875)

836. AOL

837. Paine Webber

838. Sun Microsystems

839. Exxon

840. PNC Financial Services

841. IBM

842. Disney

843. Chrysler Corporation

844. Executing the first Internet stock trade

845. 1985

846. 2001

847. 1971

848. Insider trading

849. Ameritrade

850. BP oil spill

851. Coca-Cola and PepsiCo

852. Jacques Nasser

853. Wellington Fund

854. Levi Strauss & Co.

855. Founders of *The Wall Street Journal*

856. Massachusetts Investors' Trust

857. SBC Communications

858. Fiat

859. JPMorgan Chase

860. Barings Bank

861. Gold Reserve Act

862. Intel

863. 1987

864. Gillette (now a brand of Procter & Gamble)

865. Morgan Stanley

866. Sallie Mae

867. Standard & Poor's

868. 1984

869. 1929 (sold for $625,000 or over $6 million today)

870. Chinese Gong (before that a gavel)

871. 1973

872. FDIC

873. Continentals

874. Confederate securities

875. False, they were installed much earlier in 1878.

876. The Credit Mobilier Scandal

877. Massachusetts Bay Colony

878. General Motors

879. Scottsdale Securities

880. Orange County, California

881. London Stock Exchange

882. Marvel Entertainment (now a subsidiary of Disney)

883. Daimler Benz

884. Philadelphia Stock Exchange

885. Morgan Stanley

886. General Motors

887. 30.57 points (or about 11.7%)

888. Transition to real-time quotes (from 20-minute delayed quotes)

889. 1914 (caused by the start of WWI)

890. 1934

891. 1995

892. Sugarcane processing

893. Des Plaines, Illinois

894. No-load mutual fund

895. Commercial banking and investment banking

896. Options

897. Cable News Network (CNN)

898. Opened the first all-female owned brokerage firm

899. Joseph Schlitz Brewing Company

**900.** Visa (IPO in 2008)

**901.** General Motors

**902.** Morgan Stanley

**903.** Merrill Lynch

**904.** Alcoa

**905.** Remington Rand (acquired by Sperry Corporation, then merged with Burroughs to form Unisys)

**906.** American International Group

**907.** October 29, 1929

**908.** Charles Lindbergh's solo flight to Paris

**909.** Four

**910.** Toyota

**911.** Advent of World War I

**912.** 1968

**913.** Bank of America

**914.** The Dark Ages

**915.** Spalding

**916.** Two

**917.** (a) Primary

**918.** James Garfield

**919.** U.S. Leather

**920.** Scene of the United States' first presidential inauguration when George Washington took the oath of office

**921.** F. W. Woolworth Company

**922.** Chemical Bank

**923.** AOL

**924.** United States Rubber Company

**925.** Mazda

**926.** Penn Central

**927.** Twitter

**928.** President Andrew Jackson

**929.** 14,164.53 (set on October 9, 2007)

**930.** Texas Coffee Company

**931.** First hedge fund

**932.** About half of the 1929 level

**933.** T-Mobile USA

**934.** General Motors

**935.** Unocal

**936.** Barclay's

**937.** General Electric (since 1907)

**938.** Fannie Mae (1999 to 2004)

**939.** Leonard "Dennis" Kozlowski

**940.** Amaranth Advisors

**941.** PepsiCo

**942.** Alexander Hamilton

**943.** Dot.com or tech

**944.** Chapter 11

945. Alcoa

946. Long-Term Capital Management

947. Standard & Poor's

948. (c) Mutual Funds

949. Lucent Technologies

950. Goldman Sachs

951. Oliver Stone

952. Bull and bear

953. 17th-century (in 1653)

954. Consumer News and Business Channel

955. Delaware

956. Priceline.com

957. Himself, Charlie Sheen

958. Michael Douglas

959. News

960. The Roaring Twenties

961. *Trading Places*

962. Pigs

963. True

964. Good

965. Labor Hall of Fame

966. The University of Michigan

967. *Financial Times*

968. *Investor's Business Daily*

969. RJR Nabisco

970. Equifax

971. True

972. Post 9

973. Cuban cigars

974. Chartered Financial Analyst

975. *The Wall Street Journal*

976. Save Our Saucepans

977. Pat Riley, who at that time was head coach of the Los Angeles Lakers

978. Cocaine spoons

979. Series 6

980. Trend

981. Entertainment and Sports Programming Network

982. 50-day

983. Orange juice

984. Heard

985. *Mad Money*

986. *American Greed*

987. Harvard and Yale

988. Thursdays (at 8:30am ET)

989. Non-farm payrolls and unemployment rate

990. White Knight

991. Tom Cruise

992. Cassa

993. $500 bill

994. Board of Directors

**995.** *Fortune*

**996.** Maryland at 7.22%

**997.** *American Psycho*

**998.** Positively correlated

**999.** Daryl Hannah

**1000.** Dow Jones & Company, Inc.

**1001.** Humphrey Bogart

This book is available
for purchase
as a print or eBook.

www.ingramcontent.com/pod-product-compliance
Lightning Source LLC
Chambersburg PA
CBHW031320040426
42443CB00005B/153